D0211355

HOCKEY'S HOT STOVE

HOCKEY'S
HOT STOVE

The Untold Stories of the
Original Insiders

Al Strachan

Published by SIMON & SCHUSTER
New York   London   Toronto   Sydney   New Delhi

Simon & Schuster Canada
A Division of Simon & Schuster, Inc.
166 King Street East, Suite 300
Toronto, Ontario M5A 1J3

This Simon & Schuster Canada edition December 2020

SIMON & SCHUSTER CANADA and colophon are
trademarks of Simon & Schuster, Inc.

For information about special discounts for bulk purchases,
please contact Simon & Schuster Special Sales at 1-800-268-3216
or CustomerService@simonandschuster.ca.

Manufactured in the United States of America

1   3   5   7   9   10   8   6   4   2

Library and Archives Canada Cataloguing in Publication
Title: Hockey's hot stove : the untold stories of the original insiders / Al Strachan.
Names: Strachan, Al, author.
Description: Simon & Schuster Canada edition
Identifiers: Canadiana (print) 20200208160 |
Canadiana (ebook) 20200208179 | ISBN 9781982147013 (hardcover) |
ISBN 9781982147020 (ebook)
Subjects: LCSH: Hockey night in Canada (Television program) |
LCSH: Hockey—Anecdotes. |
LCSH: National Hockey League—Anecdotes.
Classification: LCC GV742.3 .S77 2020 | DDC 070.4/497969620971—dc23

ISBN 978-1-9821-4701-3
ISBN 978-1-9821-4702-0 (ebook)

This one is for Penny, who I think of every day

Contents

CONTENTS

Ground Rules

When *Hot Stove* came on the air, the hockey world stopped. In every press box where Canadian teams were playing, there was a stampede towards the TV monitors. Columnists, reporters, and broadcasters left their laptops at their workstations and dashed to hear what was being said.

In the western Canadian arenas, where the teams had just warmed up for the second game of the Saturday-night doubleheader on *Hockey Night in Canada*, the players gathered around the dressing-room televisions. For a while, the timing and duration of pregame preparation had varied. But before long, players were demanding that pregame skates be coordinated with the TV schedule. NHL players, it seems, were as fascinated by hockey gossip as everyone else.

In the coaches' rooms and in the general managers' offices, it was the same story. *Satellite Hot Stove* was required viewing. It was the *Hockey Night in Canada* segment that could not be missed. Even the on-ice officials—the referees and linesmen—were glued to the TV in their dressing rooms.

And most important, in living rooms across Canada, a cone of silence descended. It was time to catch up on the inside news from around the league. The younger kids had been put to bed, and the older ones could be counted upon to follow orders and keep quiet for eight minutes.

The show had various names. Sometimes it was *Satellite Hot Stove* or *Hot Stove by Satellite*, or simply, *Hot Stove*. Sometimes it was *After 40 Minutes* or just plain *After 40*. To avoid confusion, I'll generally refer to the show throughout the book as *Hot Stove*, even though, at the moment in question, the tall foreheads at the CBC might have decided to present it under another name. Whatever the show was called, the idea was always the same. In the second intermission of the first game on *Hockey Night in Canada*, media "insiders" would reveal to viewers what was going on in hockey's secret world.

Because the show aired once a week, the myriad *Hockey Night in Canada* employees who put it together (it was, after all, a CBC production in those days and therefore overstaffed) had plenty of time to try to justify their presence. That's why there was always tinkering.

Names changed. Faces changed. Intros changed. The music changed. The sponsors changed. Even executive producers changed. People were fired [puts up hand]. People were brought back [puts up hand, again]. But for more than a decade, with only a few short-lived aberrations, the idea never changed. Tell the viewers what they didn't already know. Give them information they couldn't get anywhere else.

The move to Sportsnet in 2014 changed all that. The second intermission on Saturday became, for the most part, a few people discussing the news from Tuesday or telling you what you had just seen during the game. It gradually got better, but its early productions were not riveting, to say the least. A small part of the show might have involved breaking news, but that was no longer the primary focus.

Did the original *Hot Stove* enrage some hockey people? Yes, it did, without a doubt. But it was always my feeling that I didn't work for the people we were talking about during the telecast. We worked for the viewers, and as a result, I occasionally said things that were almost certain to create what might politely be referred to as feedback, but which often took the form of obscenity-laden phone calls.

But I always believed I was telling the truth, and if it angered some people, so be it. That's the approach I intend to take in this book as well. There will be those who don't like what I say about them. My response is simple and the same as it was during *Hot Stove*: I'm sorry, but at the moment, you're not my priority.

There are less delicate ways to phrase that sentiment, and in conversation I often use those four-letter words. Sometimes, they will pop up in this book—mostly when I'm quoting someone. Hockey players have a language all their own. When they talk about sharking, it has nothing to do with fish. It refers to cruising around back and forth in the area in front of the net. When they talk about flow, it's a hairdo. They have many others. But the one prevailing word in their language is the same one that is in common use almost everywhere these days: it is "fuck."

There's no sense bothering with asterisks. If I write s**t or a**hole, you all know what the word is. Why bother? So, I'm going to use the words when they occur naturally. If you don't like that kind of language, I apologize. But the reality is that any reflection of the genuine hockey world has to include some words that were once considered reprehensible but are now standard parts of any movie, book, HBO documentary, or conversation involving teenage girls. If you have any doubts about the language that hockey players routinely use, go back and look at the postgame televised interviews with the St. Louis Blues after they won the 2019 Stanley Cup. I'm just preparing you for it now.

To those who say, "You didn't use that word on television," I have to say sorry, but you're wrong. You probably didn't notice because at the time John Davidson, one of my longtime compatriots on the show, was shouting over me—a not uncommon occurrence—and nobody heard it. But it definitely did slip out once. I said, "Oh, for fuck's sake," during one of Davidson's pro–Gary Bettman speeches. (I wasn't the only one thinking it, but I was the only one to say it.)

I must admit, though, that at the time, in that earlier era, I was horrified at what I had just done. It was around 1998, and the reaction to it in those days was considerably different to what it is today. I knew that if the wrong people had noticed, I was probably doing my last show. Anyway, I won't use it gratuitously in this book, but if it fits, or if it's part of a quote, you'll see it.

I was once told that conversations with me were like those paddle toys with a rubber ball attached by an elastic. The ball flies off in an unpredictable direction, but it always comes back. We all do that, don't we? We start to tell a story, then say, "That reminds me," and relate another anecdote before getting back to where we were. Over the years, I've spent many an hour having a beer or two with people who wanted me to tell them about my experiences. They all seemed to enjoy it, so it's my intention to produce a book that is a lot like a chat in a pub over a few pints.

This book is, after all, written for hockey fans, so it will take the form of a hockey conversation among friends. Sometimes it will wander a bit, just as conversations among friends do. But don't worry, after being interrupted by an anecdote (or maybe two) it will eventually get back to the discussion at hand.

You can count on honesty here, but I must admit that once in a while, you may encounter an anecdote that you have heard before. If I'm going to give you as much insight as possible into the inner workings of *Hot Stove*, I will have to occasionally use some information that appeared in earlier books.

Also, on rare occasions, I may not choose to identify the central characters in a story. For instance, the Toronto Maple Leafs once traded for a skilled player (I'll avoid the obvious cheap shot for once) and I mentioned to Ken Dryden, the general manager at the time, that he had acquired a guy who could be a seriously positive force. Kenny said that he was glad I felt that way. I wasn't sure whether he was being honest or sarcastic—he was highly proficient at both—but the conversation moved on, and he noted that he hadn't had to give up as much as he expected.

"That's because the team he came from had to get him off their roster in a hurry," I explained. "He had an affair with the wife of that guy they just traded for, and they had to get him out of the room before the other guy showed up." Dryden admitted that he hadn't known that. I assured him that even though it was true, the story would go no further. It wouldn't appear in my *Toronto Sun* newspaper columns and it wouldn't be discussed on *Hot Stove*.

There are some stories you just don't make public when they're hot, but you can still use them to explain a set of circumstances. Collecting gossip is a lot like being a commercial fisherman. When you haul in your net, you never know what you might have dredged up.

When I refer to gossip, I don't mean the malicious, nasty whispers that are meant to be hurtful. I'm just talking about the kind of chatter that is exchanged throughout the National Hockey League—various insights, rumours, speculation, that sort of thing.

At times, the *Hot Stove* segment of *Hockey Night in Canada* pulled in the highest rating of the week for Canadian television. Someone had tipped me off about this, but when I asked one of the upper management people about it, he was quite evasive. I continued to talk to him about it (badgered him might also be an acceptable description) and he admitted that this was indeed the case. He then pleaded with me to keep quiet about it because mentioning it might upset Don Cherry, who was convinced that his *Coach's Corner* segment in the first intermission always topped the weekly ratings. And no one wanted to upset Don Cherry.

Personally, I doubt very much that Don would have been upset. We were both part of *Hockey Night in Canada*, after all, and having it lead the ratings race would be Don's primary concern. Nevertheless, it was not a matter we ever discussed.

When it came to the matter of content on *Hot Stove*, honesty was generally encouraged, and we were free to take a swipe at anybody— at least in the early going, while John Shannon was the executive producer.

My memories of my time on *Hockey Night in Canada* fall into two categories. There was the period when Shannon was there and the period when he wasn't. To me, the former was by far the better. John always looked upon himself as working for the fans, not for the corporate minions at CBC. To him, and to me, the show was a lot better that way.

Certainly, he had to field complaints, but those complaints were mostly from people within the hockey community who felt we had slaughtered a few of their sacred cows or failed to exhibit the levels of adulation they felt they deserved. The viewers seemed to love it.

On the inside, it was never the same after John left. The show still went on but it kept changing its approach. It moved away from being an irreverent, over-the-backyard-fence, scattershot exchange of gossip and became more of a sanitized hockey panel, expressing moderate opinions that the new management considered to be more in line with NHL-approved views.

We were encouraged to make some ever-so-slight modifications. We were still free to take a swipe at anybody—anybody who wasn't one of management's sacred cows, that is. And as long as we didn't disparage the Leafs or Canadiens. And as long as we were suitably politically correct at all times. And as long as we weren't too strident in our criticism. And as long as no one was likely to call to complain. The level of reverence that was supposed to be accorded to the various spheres of influence depended on who was in charge of the show at the moment and where that person's particular interests might lie.

I suppose that's probably the case in all businesses, but you might not expect that at the Canadian Broadcasting Corporation, where the inherent commitment to integrity is constantly trumpeted, and the truth presumably all that was needed.

Too often, it wasn't.

CHAPTER 1

In the Beginning,
1994–2000

Who created *Satellite Hot Stove*? There is a straightforward answer, but you could also dig a little deeper and look at motivating factors. In simple terms, John Shannon was the *Hot Stove*'s heavenly father—or its Dr. Frankenstein, depending on how you feel about the show. But the two people who created the conditions for its genesis were Wayne Gretzky and National Hockey League commissioner Gary Bettman. Without the involvement of those two, it might never have happened.

The story goes back to June 1994. The New York Rangers won the Stanley Cup and suddenly the NHL was poised for an unprecedented surge in popularity. The Rangers had taken New York, the media capital of the world, by storm. The franchise hadn't won the Cup since 1940, a fact that New York Islanders fans repeatedly reminded them of by chanting that date whenever the Rangers played in Long Island.

But in the minds of those who lived in the teeming boroughs of Manhattan, Queens, and the Bronx, the Islanders weren't really a New York team. They played in Uniondale, on Long Island, in Nassau County. They might as well have been in New Jersey. Even though the Islanders had won four consecutive Stanley Cups starting in 1980, they had never really captured the hearts of the city. They were an expansion team. The Rangers were one of the Original Six.

I covered every Rangers playoff game that year, and since the Madison Square Garden press box is in the middle of the stands, I got to make some acquaintances among the season ticket holders who sat right behind my press-box seat.

They were stereotypical New Yorkers: brash, demanding, and occasionally obscene. But when the Rangers finally won the Cup, in game seven against the Vancouver Canucks, two of them were crying. Crying!

"I never thought I'd live to see this day," blubbered one, as his buddy nodded in agreement, with tears rolling down his cheeks.

The Rangers' road to the Cup had been dominating the news for weeks. Mike Keenan was coaching the team, and Mark Messier was its captain—two people who knew very well how to ride the crest of the media wave. After the championship, New York was in love with the Rangers.

So when it was time to start the next season—time to capitalize on this torrent of emotion and exploit the New York media to finally award the NHL the major-sport status it had craved for so long—Bettman responded decisively. He shut down the league.

He locked out the players in a salary dispute. When NHL training camps should have been starting and fans were eagerly anticipating more hockey, the National Football League got rolling. Not long afterwards, baseball started its playoffs. Still, no hockey. Soon the fans had turned their attention to other sports, and the NHL's New York glory was a distant memory. The league was once again relegated to also-ran status.

About a month after the lockout began, I was on a cross-country flight with Gretzky, his teammate Marty McSorley, and Gretzky's agent Mike Barnett. There was hardly anyone else in business class, so we huddled together and proceeded to work on a concept Gretzky had devised.

To help pass some time during the lockout, he would put together a team of NHLers and stage a goodwill tour of Scandinavia. It would proceed with the understanding that if a settlement were to be reached between the NHL and the NHL Players' Association, the tour would end immediately.

We talked about the itinerary, the logistics, and the personnel. As we came up with names of potential participants, Barnett phoned them using the ridiculously expensive telephones (twelve dollars U.S. per minute or part thereof, if I remember rightly) that were in the seatbacks of airplanes in those days.

Some players were delighted to accept. Others couldn't for one reason or another. Doug Gilmour, for example, would have loved to play, but he was committed to Rapperswil-Jona, a team in Switzerland. The team was sponsored by a local radio station, so Gilmour wore number 107.4, the station's frequency on the FM dial.

We also called Mario Lemieux, even though we hadn't thought of him at first because he was out of hockey at the time, recuperating from a form of cancer. Like Gilmour, he, too, would have loved to join the tour, and he felt healthy enough. But his doctors advised against it and his insurance company forbade it.

Loyal to the tried-and-true standards followed by agents throughout the generations, Barnett used his client's credit card to make all these calls. Long-distance charges were always hefty in those days, even if they were made from the ground. "I pay my dad's phone bills," chuckled Gretzky as he waited for Barnett to wrap up another call. "He pays Bell Canada more for long-distance charges now than he was paid by that company when he worked for them." Nevertheless, the expenditure paid dividends. By the time we landed in Los Angeles, what started as a vague idea had become a firm plan.

The next time I was on a plane with Gretzky, it was December 1, and we were heading from Detroit to Helsinki, Finland, with Gretzky's touring team, the 99 All-Stars. The Scandinavian goodwill tour was a go.

The team had held a two-day training camp in Auburn Hills, Michigan, culminating with a game against the Detroit Vipers of the International Hockey League. Three of the Gretzky all-stars, Steve Yzerman, Paul Coffey, and Sergei Fedorov, sat out the game because they all played for the Detroit Red Wings at the time and it wasn't Gretzky's intention to create any animosity with the NHL.

Even so, they were in the rink that night and nothing could have made John Shannon happier than the presence of so many great NHL players in one arena. By that time, he was desperate. He had been named executive producer of *Hockey Night in Canada* during the summer, but Bettman had shut down the season.

"We needed programming badly," John recalled. "We ran some classic games in the Saturday-night time slot but we felt that the most important thing to do was update everybody on the lockout. That's when we started to use guys like Scott Morrison, Jim Kelley, John Davidson, and Jim Hughson to give us updates and discuss the issues of what players and owners were dealing with. They all appeared on *Satellite Hot Stove* later."

Gretzky's Scandinavian goodwill tour did indeed turn out to be a godsend for Shannon. First of all, he sent a crew to Detroit to get footage to use in the coming non-NHL-hockey weeks. Also, he made arrangements to have two of the games scheduled for Saturdays, so they could have a same-day telecast in North America.

And to add more authenticity, Bob Cole and Harry Neale, the "A-team" broadcasters on the CBC telecast, joined the entourage. Even Ron MacLean came along to give the production a full *Hockey Night in Canada* appearance, despite the fact that it was Hockey Night in Finland the first time and Hockey Night in Sweden the next time.

"And when Gretz went on with Ron after the first period of that first game, you got him to wear a hat plugging that bar you partly owned in Toronto," said Shannon, reminding me of one of the many business ventures I've been trying hard to forget.

It should have been mainly vacation for MacLean with six off-days between games, but he lost his passport and had to spend most of the time pulling strings and visiting Canadian embassies across Scandinavia to get an immediate replacement. He also disappeared from a pub in Oslo, Norway, one night in the company of a very strange-looking couple. By closing time, he still hadn't returned, thereby generating some (mild) concern among the rest of us. We still haven't figured out how he came to be sleeping in the back of the bus that picked us up at our hotel the next morning. We would have asked him, but he was sound asleep, and by the time he woke up, no one cared anymore.

The second intermission in both televised European games was dedicated to lockout updates, and that's when it all came together for Shannon. The public response to the telecasts during the lockout made it clear to him that there was a craving for hockey news that didn't necessarily relate directly to the game being shown. People were eager for information pertaining to hockey in general.

By the time the shortened NHL season began on January 20, 1995, Shannon had put together an entirely new version of *Hockey Night in Canada*. "We changed the world, Al," he said with a laugh.

From that point on, *Hockey Night in Canada* would no longer begin at 8 p.m. Now it would start at 7 p.m. That was necessary to accommodate another of Shannon's innovations. There wouldn't just be one game. There would be a doubleheader, with the second game starting at 10 p.m.

And every Saturday, in the second intermission of the first game, there would be this split-screen show with little boxes containing talking heads and these heads would give you snippets of information about what had happened, what was happening, and what was going to happen in the hockey world.

Satellite Hot Stove had been born.

CHAPTER 2

The Name Game

For a long time, I had no problem with computers. If anything went wrong, I followed an infallible two-step solution. Step one was to teach the offending machine a lesson by punching and cursing it. This rarely had any effect, of course, but I was sufficiently technologically adept to expect that. After all, a two-step solution is likely to require two steps. Step two was to shout, "IAN!" At that point, my younger son would get off his computer, come bouncing down from his room, and fix my problem in three seconds. Voila!

Naturally, this three-second performance was followed by an eye roll, a sigh, and a head shake—and a quick departure for upstairs. Ian was a teenager, after all. But it got the job done. Ian is now a professional computer geek in Boston, however, so my infallible two-step solution no longer works.

The technology is improving rapidly, though, and I find life easier with a new iPad. I selected the one with the largest available memory so that I can watch movies (I don't know how to load movies into it, of course, but will someday). This machine does a lot of things; it even talks to me, and I quickly figured out that my iPad is a female. And judging by her accent, she's an American.

But then I briefly loaned the iPad to my granddaughter Vivienne, who lives in England. She was six at the time. Now my iPad is male, speaks with an English accent, and calls me Vivienne every time it responds. I have no idea how that came about.

I mention all this to illustrate the gap between the generations. I have tremendous admiration for the younger one. They can do so many things that I can't do (or undo), and in many cases, can't even comprehend. But at the same time, there are understandable gaps in their knowledge.

That's a typically long-winded explanation of my rationalization for discussing how *Satellite Hot Stove* got its name. If you're a part of my generation, or close to it, much of this chapter may seem obvious. But a remarkably large segment of the younger generation has asked me over the years what the name means. There were also some in that group who simply announced that they considered it stupid because it made no sense. So here we go.

Central heating is relatively new in Canada. Most of us are accustomed to living in houses that are warm, no matter what the outside temperature might be. But back when *Hockey Night in Canada* started on the radio in 1931 and everybody in the country used Fahrenheit, houses were not centrally heated. Nor were stores or restaurants. This was true even when the televised version of *Hockey Night in Canada* was in its infancy, in 1952.

The source of heat in many buildings at that time was a woodstove (a wood-burning stove, but no one called them that). In a home, this stove would be in the kitchen. In stores, restaurants, saloons, pool halls, barbershops, and other places where the public gathered, the woodstove would probably be in the centre of the room. This is why kitchen parties became such an integral part of Canadian society. The kitchen was the only warm room in the house. There were no supermarkets in that era, just general stores, and one stove would provide all the heat you were going to get.

Given the severity of Canadian winters, the woodstove tended to draw a crowd. These stoves could be of different shapes, but the most popular were potbellied, so called because their sides were convex rather than straight, in order to increase the surface area of hot metal and therefore the amount of heat it gave off.

They were, of course, quite dangerous and any child who touched the side would get a nasty burn. I once pointed this out to someone who grew up in that generation. She agreed but added, "Yes, but they only ever did it once." Apparently, it was a rite of passage.

Life tended to be a bit slower in those days and people would take time to chat, rather than look at their cell phones like today. In kitchens, and even some stores, people would pull up chairs to sit around the stove and share their views and gossip.

When Foster Hewitt started broadcasting Toronto Maple Leafs games on radio he spoke into a telephone and his voice was broadcast over a local radio station owned by the *Toronto Star*. This newfangled concept of broadcasting hockey games proved to be so popular that by 1933 it was big business. MacLaren Advertising Agency had sewn up Canadian NHL rights, signed sponsors, and formed a network of twenty stations around Canada that carried live English-language broadcasts from both Toronto and Montreal.

As more and more listeners tuned in, it became apparent that intermission content could also be sold to advertisers. Therefore, in 1939, a separate show was aired between periods with Bee Hive corn syrup as its main sponsor. It was given an ideal name for its era. The image of men sitting around a hot stove talking about hockey would resonate with everyone, and thus the "Hot Stove League" was born. Use of the word "league" made a reference to hockey while at the same time gently poking fun at men (no women would have been involved in this activity in those days) who weren't good enough to play in the NHL but had all the answers to whatever plagued it.

The guy who dreamed up the concept and the name was C. M. Passmore. (Have you noticed that hockey seems to draw an inordinate number of people who prefer initials to names?) C. M. stopped into the office only briefly in the mornings, then spent the rest of the day at a nearby tavern drinking beer and working on what had evolved into *Hockey Night in Canada*. That name had come into being at some point in the 1930s, but no one is sure exactly when.

Passmore brought in a few of his friends to form the original Hot Stove panel. One was Elmer Ferguson, the former sports editor of the *Montreal Herald*. When I worked at the *Montreal Gazette*, some of my colleagues had worked with Ferguson and told me that he always prided himself on knowing how much to charge for including something in the newspaper. It was a form of graft that accrued to sports editors in those days.

One day, a farmer from Quebec's south shore, wearing ragged, muddy coveralls, came in with a picture of his local curling team and a short story detailing their recent success. He wanted some coverage. Ferguson assured him that he could get it—for a small fee, of course. The farmer agreed, and asked how much it would be. Ferguson looked him up and down, saw the mud, saw the ragged clothes, and made his appraisal. He didn't want to drive the man off, but he wanted the maximum. "Twenty-five dollars," he said.

"No problem," replied the farmer as he pulled a large wad of bills out of his pocket.

"And two hundred dollars for the picture," added Ferguson, instantly.

I heard that story a number of times in Montreal, so naturally, there were some slight variations. But I was assured that the basis of it was factual.

If you're a sportswriter today and you get selected for the media wing of the Hockey Hall of Fame, you are accorded a further honour. You are given the Elmer Ferguson Award, representative of excellence in sports journalism. I will make no further comment on the irony of that, especially since, like almost everyone else who ever covered hockey for a Toronto paper, I once got the award.

Also on the panel of that original Hot Stove League: former Leafs player Harold "Baldy" Cotton, sportswriter Bobby Hewitson from the now long-defunct *Toronto Telegram*, and Wes McKnight from CFRB Radio in Toronto. They were almost as important as the game itself and as highly regarded as the players. There aren't many people still around who were listening to hockey on the radio in the 1940s. But if you know one, ask him if he remembers Fergy, Baldy, Bobby, and Wes. He might tear up. He'll certainly smile. Those four were an institution in a long-gone age.

But like so many shows that were a rage on radio, the *Hot Stove League* couldn't make a successful transition to television. In 1952, *Hockey Night in Canada* did make the transition, but although the *Hot Stove League* took up most of the second intermission, it had lost its mystique.

Two members of the radio panel refused to leave the relative anonymity of radio and were replaced by former players who were there not because of what they were, but because of what they had been (a practice of dubious merit that is not unknown in television today). One of these was Ted "Teeder" Kennedy, a former Leafs captain. The other was Syl Apps, who was required to start each show by shoving a piece of wood into the fake potbellied stove on the set that had been built for the new black-and-white television version of the *Hot Stove League.*

It didn't help that the set was in a separate building a five-minute walk from Maple Leaf Gardens. If the most interesting play of the game so far occurred in the last five minutes of the second period, the participants would, of course, be expected to discuss it. But they wouldn't have seen it, and replays did not exist at that time.

Before long, the *Hot Stove League* was killed off and replaced by a series of terminally boring filler shows. My personal favourite was the one where *Toronto Sun* sports editor George Gross, who was occasionally used to fill time between periods with pieces that had some vague relationship to hockey, pointed out what he claimed was a rock garden in Japan. Unfortunately for the show's reputation—and George's—the Japanese rock garden was adjacent to large windows in an office building. And in those windows was the clear reflection of a Toronto streetcar passing by.

In 1995, when John Shannon brought back his variation on the Hot Stove theme in a new age of split-screen television, he embraced the tradition but reminded viewers that this was a modern version. It was not the *Hot Stove League*, it was *Satellite Hot Stove*.

"To me, the name was a tribute to the old Hot Stove," Shannon explained to me one day. "When you're running a show that had been on radio and TV since the 1930s, you had to show some respect for what was there. The old Hot Stove on radio had morphed to TV in the fifties—and was all scripted, by the way. The show you were on was far from scripted."

That's certainly true. People who listened to the original *Hot Stove League* were invariably impressed by the wit, intelligence, and insight shown by the participants. Those of us on the new version of the show may not have been so polished, but we were saying whatever came into our heads, not what had been written for us.

When C. M. Passmore sat in the pub all day, he wasn't just drinking beer, he was also writing the scripts for the *Hot Stove League*. The interruptions, the droll observations, and the "ad libs" were all in the script.

For one thing, that's the way things were generally done on network radio in those days. But furthermore, when World War II began, everything that went out over the CBC airwaves had to be censored. The wartime censor even had his own office in the CBC building. It wasn't quite that bad for us, but Shannon never let us toss out personal messages because the show was for the viewers, not for our friends or relatives.

Similarly, personal messages were banned from the precursor radio version as well, albeit for a different reason. If Baldy or Fergy were to take a moment to say, "Happy Birthday to my nephew whose regiment is fighting in the heat in North Africa," it could be seen as giving the enemy information of military activities. Loose lips sink ships, and all that.

We were never told what to say or how to say it. We were on our own and although some producers might insist on more structure, Shannon wasn't one of them. "It didn't matter," he said. "As long as it was entertaining and informative, we were okay as far as I was concerned."

CHAPTER 3

Live on Tape

We always called it "the Circus." I have no idea who came up with the name. Nor does anyone else, it seems. But I figure it comes from the days before the CBC studio became available and we used to move around a lot to do the show out of various arenas. Someone probably referred to it as a travelling circus, and the name stuck.

In fact, "the Circus" could be used as a catchall name for the entire *Hockey Night in Canada* package, but more often, the staffer who used it was making a reference to *Hot Stove*—and not necessarily a flattering one. The show was definitely mobile. Ron MacLean was always the host, and he would usually have at least one other participant with him. But there was no telling where the others might be located.

In the early days, we tended to tape the shows at 3 p.m. There were a couple of reasons for this. One was the regular presence on the show of John Davidson. Throughout the rest of the book, he will be referred to as JD, as is invariably the case in the real world. I have known him since dirt was invented and could count on one hand the number of times I have heard someone call him John.

When P. J. Stock made some appearances on the show years later, I used to refer to him as Philip, just to annoy him. P. J. is one of those people you just feel you have to annoy. Hang around with him for a while and see how many people deliberately try to annoy him. And you'll find out why. It's not just me. I must say, though, that he gives as good as he gets, so even though he might be annoying, he's also good company. But JD was always JD, never John. I used to annoy him, too, but I did it in a different way and rarely intentionally. He is—and always has been—one of my favourite people, in hockey or out of it.

JD was the colour guy on the New York Rangers telecasts on the MSG Network, and like most NHL teams, the Rangers played a lot of Saturday-night games. So to accommodate JD's other job, we had to tape our show in the afternoon.

We all had other jobs, of course, and this was truly the golden age of sports journalism. I think most of us realized it. We were able to travel to all the major sporting events, and much to the disgust of other sections of the paper, it was the sports department that was allocated the lion's share of the budget.

It wasn't all perfect. As Scott Morrison, then one of the *Toronto Sun*'s hockey writers, pointed out when we were strolling around London, England, the year the Toronto Maple Leafs played a couple of exhibition games there, "This would be a great job if we didn't have to write." It was a concept that we discussed over a pint in the next pub we came across.

Involvement in *Hot Stove* was also more fun than work. If I happened to be in the same town as the Circus, mostly Toronto or Montreal, I would go to the studio, but those were the days when major newspapers had lots of money and understood the importance of sports, so I was often in some far-flung locale.

Just to give you an idea of the way things were, when I started at the *Globe and Mail* in September 1980, the annual sports department budget was whatever the sports department spent. I had been there only a couple of months when, in a rare burst of long-range planning, the managing editor called me into the east wing of his cavernous office and asked if I would be interested in covering the National Football League the following season.

That sounded like a decent idea to me. I had a great deal of NFL knowledge I was eager to impart and, as a Detroit Lions fan, was

excited about covering their impending Super Bowl victory in 1982—
or 1983, at the latest.

"Then you'd better go to the annual NFL meeting," said the managing editor.

"Okay. I guess so. Where is it?"

"Maui."

"Maui? The Maui in Hawaii? That Maui? Well, I guess I should. It is, after all, my new beat so I guess it's my responsibility. And you'll surely never find anyone else willing to do it. I'll make the sacrifice."

I didn't say that last part out loud. But the rest of the conversation is accurate and the *Globe and Mail* did indeed send me to Maui. I was there for six days, and on three of them, they decided that they already had plenty of news to fill the available space so I shouldn't bother writing.

Nevertheless, I was dedicated to my craft. There was no sense wasting a day, and since the nearby Royal Ka'anapali Golf Course is a regular stop on the LPGA tour, it made sense to put in a round there. I did it only to familiarize myself in case I had to cover women's golf, of course. It was purely coincidental that the round, with all the necessary accoutrements, was provided by the NFL.

A further rationalization ("fantasy" is also acceptable) was that I actually might have to cover LPGA golf. Not much time had elapsed since a *Globe and Mail* writer covering the LPGA was seen running for his life to get away from a golfer brandishing her putter and screaming obscenities at him. Maybe I would be pressed into duty because he certainly wasn't going back to that beat. In fact, the paper had sent him to the Washington bureau in the hope that he would cause less trouble in the United States than he had in Canada.

But back to the managing editor. He wasn't finished. "Since baseball training camps will have opened by the time you leave Hawaii," he said, "you might as well stop in the Phoenix area for a couple of weeks and do some stuff on the Cactus League." In that era, only four major-league baseball teams held their training camps in Arizona. They were the San Francisco Giants, Oakland A's, Chicago Cubs, and Milwaukee Brewers. To me, there did not seem to be an overwhelming demand in Canada for information on any of these teams. There was probably no demand for insight, either, which was just as well since I didn't have any.

Nevertheless, even though it might have been a burden for me to continue to bask in the desert warmth and avoid another fourteen days of Toronto weather in March, I decided to agree with the managing editor. After all, he got his job by knowing the newspaper business. Who was I, as a mere columnist, to argue? It was another sacrifice I was prepared to make for the paper.

Needless to say, the concept of spending freely, perhaps even haphazardly, on a large staff no longer prevails at the *Globe and Mail*. In fact, it no longer prevails at any traditional newspaper in North America, although a couple of them do try to avoid total submission to the popular trend of drastically chopping budgets. The *Globe* isn't one of them. When I was there, there were forty-four staffers in the sports department. Today there are four. And they rarely make road trips.

It was very different in those halcyon days and that is why I was often in a place other than Toronto when we were taping *Hot Stove*. How John Shannon and his crew dredged up the places we used in some of those remote locales, I do not know. On Friday, I'd get a phone call from one of John's minions telling me they'd found a place I needed to get to in time to do the Saturday 3 p.m. taping.

"Got a pen?"

"Yep."

"Ready?"

"Yep."

"It's called Bob's Organic TV Studio and Lawn Care."

"Is it a big place?"

"Not very. And Bob suggests that you give yourself ample time. A lot of cabdrivers don't like to go to that part of town, so it may take a while to find one who'll take you."

Usually they were good enough to provide an address. But if you're in Denver, say, and you're given an address, you have no idea how long it takes to get there from the Marriott. And since 3 p.m. in Toronto is

1 p.m. in Denver, there's the additional problem of getting up on time. Sportswriters are not generally known as early risers, and if you're in a locale where it is two hours earlier than in Toronto, the bars close two hours later than in Toronto, don't they?

Anyway, I was invariably equal to the challenge. I discovered that when a little research of a logistical nature had to be done, it was usually best to do it on Friday night. People in bars tend to be surprisingly knowledgeable about their city, so that's where I went. Another sacrifice.

When Saturday came, I'd parade down the line of cabs until I found one willing to take me to the designated address, which turned out, as often as not, to be part of a run-down (sometimes very run-down) strip mall. There would be no sign for Bob's Organic TV Studio and Lawn Care. So we'd cruise up and down a couple of times, then try around the back. And there it was—a graffiti-tagged door with a small name plate saying, "Bob's."

I'd ring the buzzer (they always had a working buzzer) and in a while, the door would be opened by a portly guy with a beard, a lumberjack shirt, and long, probably unwashed, hair. He'd introduce me to his assistant, usually a young girl dressed totally in black with bits of metal sticking out of numerous parts of her body.

But I must say, these people were always nice. No matter what city it was, whenever I got to this tiny studio somewhere on the edge of civilization, they were good to me and sometimes even gave me a ride back to my hotel. And you can be sure I didn't put a fake cab receipt into the expense account. Or if I did, it would partly make up for the time when I tipped the guy who opened my cab door outside the Marriott hotel in Boston a dollar for his service. It wasn't until much later—far too late to make amends—that I realized I had given him $100. That's ninety-nine bucks I couldn't claim back. Maybe, when you're dealing with American money, mistaking a $100 bill for a $1 bill is a rite of passage, just like putting your hand on a hot stove in Canada.

Most times, finding the locale for the Saturday shoot was not a problem. But a different difficulty might arise. One year, we were in Detroit, where Scotty Bowman was coaching the Red Wings during another one of their playoff runs. One of the *Hot Stove* decision makers thought it would be a good idea to set up a camera among the second-deck seats at Joe Louis Arena. I would sit a few rows below the camera location and have my back to the ice. The backdrop would be the empty arena and the gleaming virgin ice surface.

I must admit that it did look good. And on that day, the video aspect would prove to be especially important. We had just started taping when the Zamboni came out. When the Zambonis appear during a game, they don't seem noisy because the crowd drowns them out. But they're pretty loud in an empty arena. We taped our eight-minute segment and for the whole time, the Zamboni drove around and around.

Later that evening, I ran into Al Sobotka, one of the Joe Louis employees, best known for coming out and picking up octopuses off the ice and occasionally twirling them around over his head.

"How'd your show go this afternoon?" he asked.

That seemed to be a strange question but I told him it was okay.

"Did the noise bother you?"

"Well, it didn't help, Al," I said. "What the hell were you doing resurfacing the ice at three in the afternoon?"

"Scotty saw you up there and told me to do it," he chuckled. "He said it might drown out your comments." I just laughed. More often than not, when we were doing the show from remote locations, some sort of difficulty arose. This one was mild in comparison. Furthermore, Bowman always knew how to play the media game. He knew, as well as I did, that he now owed me a favour.

JD's moonlighting wasn't the only reason the show was usually taped in its first years. Because it was being put together from as many as four sources (if all the panelists were in different locations), it was pushing the limits of the available technology at the time. We had no properly equipped base studio and just used whichever arena was home to the Circus on that day. And as an added challenge, there were usually other games taking place, and not all games get to the second intermission at the same time.

Let's say that we are doing a live show and the Ottawa Senators get through two periods fairly quickly. Now what? Do we delay the start of *Hot Stove* and wait for the games in Toronto and Quebec City to finish their second periods before we open up the four windows for the participants? We could do that, but then Ottawa wouldn't get to see the end of *Hot Stove* because the players there would be back on the ice before the show finished.

The solution was to do the show live, but tape it and run the recorded version in the other cities. In this case, Ottawa viewers would see the show live while Quebec and Toronto viewers would see the same thing a few minutes later.

That's what happens now. But in the early days of *Hot Stove*, the technology to record and roll out footage to all the networks in just a few minutes wasn't available. So for the most part, when you watched in those days it was taped a few hours before the game started. In the playoffs, you might get to see a live version because only one game was on the network, but that always made the producers nervous—and not just because it was possible that one of the participants [raises hand] might say something stupid.

Shannon remembers only too well the first time they tried it. "In the 1996 Stanley Cup final, we decided to do a *Hot Stove* from the beach," he chuckled. "Florida was playing Colorado. You and JD were in Miami and Jimmy Hughson was in Vancouver. We were working out of this little truck that had no frills and we thought it would be a good idea to put you two guys on the beach. So there you were. It's Miami in June. There are all these people on the beach wearing what you'd expect them to wear on Miami Beach in June. You two guys are in jackets and ties because that was the dress code for *Hot Stove*. JD was sweating bullets. Maybe you were, too."

I interrupted Shannon to tell him that I was, but he wasn't any more concerned about it then than he had been in 1996. He just continued with his story.

"For some reason we couldn't get the technology to work through the audio board where you can all hear each other. So I get on the phone with Jim in Vancouver. I can hear him, but no one else can. So I hooked the phone up to the speaker in the truck. That way, you and JD heard everything [through the headset microphone that a producer uses to talk to on-camera personnel] and so did everybody in the truck, even though they were trying to work at different things. I was shitting bricks because we'd spent a lot of money on it and if it hadn't worked, it would have looked silly, but we came out of it all right and nobody noticed any difference."

All of this leads us to the inescapable question. Was it better to do the show live or have it taped? Of course, when I say taped, I mean prerecorded. The days of tape are long gone and everything is now recorded digitally. But we were using videotape when *Hot Stove* was in its infancy, and it seems less cumbersome to say taped than pre-recorded. You know what I mean. If you do the show live, there is an immediacy to it. There's a tension among the participants because you know you can't take anything back. Say an unacceptable word and you're doing your last show. Make an unsupportable allegation by stumbling over your phraseology and you've got a lawsuit in your future. Express an opinion that doesn't come out properly and you're pilloried as a fool. As a result, the fear of making a mistake can lead to a level of caution that destroys spontaneity, which should be an asset of a live show.

There's also the nervousness factor. I was so nervous doing my first show that it would have been uncomfortable for viewers to watch, and embarrassing for me to have it seen. Because we were able to retape it, the levels of discomfort and embarrassment decreased. They never went away entirely, but became bearable.

Over the years, the segment used lots of sportswriters from across Canada and the United States, and it wasn't uncommon for them to show their nervousness early in the show. So we'd stop the taping, hear an encouraging word from John Shannon, and start over. If the shows had been live, the result could have been disastrous.

Even for the veterans, the taping was sometimes a godsend. Eric Duhatschek, a fellow sportswriter who has always been based in

Calgary and gradually became the show's regular western represen-tative, is a wonderful guy and a great friend of mine, but when relating a story, he likes to leave no stone unturned. That's a nice way of saying that Eric can be a bit long-winded. He won't be shocked to read this. We have often joked about it. It was no surprise, then, that his name came up when Shannon and I were discussing the pros and cons of taping.

"How many times did we stop when Eric Duhatschek opened the show and went on for ninety seconds?" John said with a laugh. "I would say, 'Eric, you're not writing a column anymore. You're on television and a thirty-second intro has to be thirty seconds, not ninety seconds.' My favourite line to him was one time when I said, 'Eric, just tell me the time; don't build me the watch.'"

"I wouldn't try to defend myself," admitted Eric. "I don't dispute that it happened. I learned a lot of things about television from John, and one of them was to be concise. At that point, I hadn't done a lot of television, but I'd done a lot of radio and radio is the opposite. The radio people want you to fill airtime. They want you to give long, expansive answers and it's my nature to give long, expansive answers. I'm not a sound-bite kind of a guy and the discipline of having to do that was something I had to learn from John, and it was challenging."

You might note that Eric said twice in one answer that he learned to be concise from John. Apparently, the lesson's impact faded over the years.

Later on, just after I left, *Hot Stove* staged regular tryouts and it was a good idea to get to your point quickly.

"Do you remember the time Dave Shoalts was there?" asked Eric. I did indeed. Shoalts was one of the *Globe and Mail*'s hockey writers, back when they had what could be called a sports department.

"He did about three minutes off the top in a monologue," Eric recalled, "and he was gone. He never appeared on it again. The next week MacLean took a shot at him. He said, 'We're out of time. Dave Shoalts took it all last week.'"

Shoalts is a funny guy who is no longer at the *Globe and Mail*. He is now a stand-up comedian who does monologues for a living. So he disputes Eric's choice of words, but he remembers the circumstances well, if not fondly.

"I was on at least once after you left," he said when we discussed the occasion, "and it was definitely a sort of audition. But it wasn't a monologue. I was on with Mike Milbury and someone else, I forget who. Milbury made a couple of bad jokes at my expense and the only other thing I remember is Ron [MacLean], of course, never brought up any of the topics we discussed beforehand.

"Sherali Najak was in charge then and they were bringing in different people like Rick Westhead (from the *Toronto Star*) and a few others, including Ian Pulver (a player agent) of all people. About a week after I was on, Sherali called me and gave me some double talk. That was the last I heard from anyone about doing the show."

Najak was a disciple of Shannon who later took over Shannon's role. I'll devote more time to his involvement with *Hot Stove* later in this book, but the important point for now is that he fully understood the principle of brevity.

"If someone goes on too long too early," Shannon often explained, "it changes the whole perspective for what the rest of the show becomes. Then everyone tries to go on long to get their share of airtime and you get four statements in eight minutes and the show is done. That's not what the *Hot Stove* was supposed to be."

The other side of the live-not-tape debate is that sometimes live television is better *because* there are no do-overs. The adrenaline rush that comes with going live can produce a potentially intemperate (and entertaining) comment that can't be removed. For example, we did one of our rare live shows during the 1998 playoffs. The powerhouse New Jersey Devils had finished first in their conference and were the choice of many hockey followers to win the Stanley Cup. But they were eliminated in the opening round by the eighth-place Ottawa Senators. As I remember it, this was such a stunning upset that we did a bonus version of *Hot Stove* right after the game.

The widely accepted view among the others was that Devils coach Jacques Lemaire would stress his notorious defensive approach even more in the following season so that the Devils could bounce back. When I was asked what Lemaire would do, I responded quickly. "He'll quit," I said flatly.

I've never seen a replay of that show so I don't know whether my expression revealed the terror that I suddenly felt. *What the hell did I just say?* I thought. *You dork. You should just have said, "You never know with a guy like him, but maybe he'll think it's not worth the bother and quit."*

Because we were live, I didn't have the opportunity to do that with more diplomacy (never known as my strong point anyway), so I just bumbled along, trying to justify my brashness, pointing out that in the past, Lemaire had walked away from a playing career and a college coaching career. But no matter how I tried to dance around it, the fact remained that Lemaire had just completed his fifth year as coach of the Devils and during that time, he had won a Stanley Cup. Coaches don't just quit after one upset.

Then Lemaire did. Six days later.

Had I been given the opportunity to retape, I would have gone much softer with my prediction (even though I'd been proved right). And the show would therefore have had less impact on the viewers, because I wouldn't have made such a memorable, flat statement. I'd just have presented his quitting as one of a number of options. I suppose this is the spot where I'm expected to moralize a bit and say that I learned my lesson. I would never again blurt out the first thing that popped into my mind. But we all know that's not true, don't we?

In the later years, when all the other early participants had moved on, the show was broadcast from the CBC studio in downtown Toronto and was almost always live. By then, technology had advanced to the point that the problem of second periods ending at different times was no longer a concern. We would start as soon as the second period ended for any of that evening's games. In that market, viewers would see the show live. In the other cities, viewers would get the somewhat oxymoronic "live-on-tape" version.

Could the viewers detect a significant difference between the earlier taped shows and the later live versions? I doubt it. There is no clear answer to the taped-versus-live debate. On any given day, one may be better than the other, but overall there's not much difference to the viewer.

The live version is a lot easier on the producers, though. No matter what happens, they have to produce only one version. And they know that the show can't be upstaged by developments that occurred between taping and airing. As long as you're convinced your panelists are the right people for the job, you're comfortable. Producers, I learned over the years, like to feel comfortable, so they strongly prefer the live version. After all, it's not their head on the block.

CHAPTER 4

Now Is the Hour

Essentially, there were two generations of *Hot Stove*, but the biggest difference between the two probably wasn't even noticed by the viewers. There were some big changes behind the cameras as well, and we'll get to those later, but for the time being, let's just stick to the technological aspects. There was the recorded version, which was done in the first few years, and there was the more recent live version.

In the formative years the show was almost always taped, with the anchor desk originating from a tiny room in the nether regions of the arena that was hosting the primary game. Ron MacLean would be there, and usually one of the participants.

In some far-distant building, the other participants waited for all the technical operations to be carried out to get us on the same screen. We waited patiently, perhaps in a superfluous dressing room somewhere, maybe one used by the local basketball team, if there was one.

The pervading aroma in those places always added to the general down-at-heel ambience. While we were sitting in our places waiting to start, I would look around and be unable to prevent certain thoughts creeping into my head: *I'm sure we look pretty spiffy sitting here, artistically made up with our neatly pressed clothes and tidy hair (I had some in those days), but if the camera ever widened its focus and panned the room, it would be an altogether different story.*

Spiffy would no longer be an appropriate word. I'm certain that's a rat hole in the wall. And I'm certain that moldy jockstrap was hanging on that same hook when we were here last year. Does that trash can ever get emptied?

At some point in the day, the *Hockey Night* crew would have found a desk suitable for two people and hung a dusty blue curtain behind it to be used as a backdrop. Ron even alluded to it one day when he was in studio with Jim Hughson, but JD and I were on location together. As the opening music of the intro faded, Ron began the show by saying, "If you're wondering what happened to Rocky Balboa's old robes, you can see one draped behind Al Strachan and John Davidson in Philadelphia."

Wherever we were, wires would have been strung around the room and stabilized (in theory) by electrical tape. If the wires were running across the floor, they were covered by yellow plastic blocks so you wouldn't trip over them. I generally tripped over the yellow plastic blocks instead. A couple of rickety stools with exceptionally slippery seats completed the package.

When we were in Maple Leaf Gardens, which was most of the time, the "studio" was a little more elegant (not a difficult goal to achieve). There we were allocated a room adjacent to the medical facilities. The talent—which is a TV word for the people in front of the camera and not necessarily a description of their attributes—the techies, a camera or two (but usually just one), a monitor, the makeup artist, the floor manager, and the occasional hanger-on would squeeze into this tiny room for the 3 p.m. festivities.

At least, they were supposed to be 3 p.m. festivities. Once in a while they weren't, and in one instance, when lateness was developing into a commonplace occurrence, it was too much for John Shannon. I happened to be in Toronto by myself that day. Don and Ron and the rest of the crew were somewhere else, probably Ottawa.

That meant that I was to be filling one of the boxes in a corner of the screen and it also meant that the transmission of my contributions had to be coordinated with the others. And in those circumstances, it definitely helps if everybody is ready to go at the projected start time.

It was about 3:03 and the sound guy was fiddling with my micro-phone, trying to duct tape it to my tie or something, when Shannon roared into the room. He was loud. Very loud. I didn't get this outburst on tape, but it was so memorable that I think what follows would be very close to verbatim.

"Let's get one fucking thing straight," he shouted to no one in particular. "The satellite window opens at three o'clock and this show starts at three o'clock. That means he [pointing at the talent] is wired up and ready to go. It means that the fucking cameras are ready. It means that all the fucking lighting is set up and operating. It means that everything is in its place and we start at fucking three o'clock. Is everybody clear on that?"

There wasn't a sound in the room. Shannon started to leave and stopped briefly by the door where Lianne Harrower was standing—or possibly cringing. Lianne handled our makeup, although we used to kid her that she might as well be putting earrings on a pig.

John didn't say a word to her, but he gave her a quick look and a slight nod to suggest that she was excluded from this particular bit of criticism, but at the same time, her continued excellence was expected.

"Yeah, Lianne always brings that up," admitted Shannon. "I remem-ber that day. I'd like to think that when I was at work, I was always passionate and prepared. My frustration came when a person didn't listen the first two times. I certainly admit I would get frustrated, but it wasn't for a lack of informing people what we were doing."

That was true. John never left any doubt as to what he expected. And occasionally, he would shout at people, as many TV producers do. One of the guys who produced the Los Angeles Kings games was notorious for outbursts that made Shannon's look like nothing more than a muttered grumble. The LA guy would scream epithets at his underlings all game long. One day, he shouted, "You're all trying to fuck me! You might as well do it properly. Here you go! Come and get me!" At this point, he dropped his trousers and underwear and bent over, still screaming instructions. Shannon didn't come close to doing any-thing like that, but he did agree that he would make sure he was heard.

"I'm a loud guy," he conceded. "My wife always tells me that I'm confrontational even when I just say, 'Hello,' on the phone. My wife says to me, 'People are afraid to phone the house in case you answer.'"

It would be a mistake to think that John was out of control when he shouted at someone. He wasn't. It just appeared that way to those who didn't know better. It's a trick I myself have used on occasion, one I learned early in my reporting career by watching Scott Bowman.

The Canadiens had lost a game in Buffalo and Bowman, the Montreal coach at the time, was of the belief that shoddy officiating was to blame. He was standing in a little hall outside the dressing room explaining this point to the media when Scotty Morrison (no relation to Scott Morrison of *Satellite Hot Stove*) walked past. Scotty was the league's referee-in-chief at the time and Bowman decided his opinion of the officiating deserved a wider audience than the Montreal media. He shouted at Morrison, not one of his favourite people, that with any sort of competent officiating his team would not have lost. Was Bowman out of control? A casual observer might think so. But was he really?

Morrison blew up and started screaming at Bowman. His face, contorted with anger, turned red. It was a shocking performance. Morrison was definitely out of control. At this point, an ice-cool Bowman jerked a thumb towards Morrison and calmly said to the press corps, "There's your referee-in-chief, boys."

Shannon knew the trick as well. "The guy I learned a little bit of that from was Herb Brooks," he said. Herb had a brilliant hockey mind and was a good friend of mine. We spoke often over the years about the course hockey was taking compared to the direction in which it should be heading. More important, Herb was the coach of the "Miracle on Ice" Team USA that won the gold medal at the 1980 Lake Placid Olympics.

"Herb was a master motivator," Shannon continued, "but he would pick out a guy to pick on. He almost made a deal with the guy: I'm going to yell at you because I know you can take it. The guy I picked on during our shows was Greg Millen. It was the farthest thing from my mind to get mad at Greg. I was really mad at everybody else. Greg would be on the verge of just telling me to go fuck myself and I'd give him a wink, then he'd catch on."

If you knew Shannon at all, you knew that his outbursts were intense but brief. Furthermore, they were not as common as they were said to be in some circles. As a powerful man in the hockey world, he was often the subject of conversations, and in such circumstances, exaggeration sometimes creeps in. I have heard people say that Shannon was always shouting at his staff. Yes, I'll admit he shouted once in a while, but it wasn't very often and I never saw him shout at someone who didn't deserve it.

"A lot of people were petrified of him," Lianne said, "but I always used to tell him, 'You don't scare *me.*' Usually, he was right about whatever he was yelling about. He was in an era where people actually knew what they were talking about and knew the way things should be done. He wasn't one of those losers who came later who don't have a clue what anything should be, and they're just yelling because they're incompetent. I always really appreciated how loyal John is and was. He could be very blustery, but I was never offended by him."

I found working for Shannon to be a treat. If you did your job properly, you had an easy life. He would tell you what he wanted—which was unquestionably his right as executive producer—so you knew what was expected. Then you did it. Where's the problem?

It must be conceded that had the reins been too tight, there would definitely have been a problem. But that was never the case. When Shannon told you what he wanted, he still left a lot of room for you to follow your own intuition.

His approach reminded me of something I was once told by John Muckler, the coach of the Edmonton Oilers in one of their Stanley Cup years. He said that as far as he was concerned, the players had some limited duties in the area of defence, but on offence they were free to try whatever they wanted. If it didn't work, it didn't work. You lost the puck and maybe, every once in a while, it cost you a goal. But the game moved on, you kept on trying to be innovative, and eventually it paid off. "An error of commission never bothers me," Muckler said. "It's the errors of omission that bother me."

Shannon was like that. You had certain limited responsibilities that mostly boiled down to being there on time and being mentally prepared. The first one was self-explanatory. The second could be loosely translated as: if you are working off a hangover, make sure you don't let it affect your performance. Other than that, there were very few rules. We were given almost total freedom to say whatever we wanted.

He snapped at me once—and only once—and it was far from a tirade. It was my elder son's birthday and Shannon was producing the show. That meant that at any time, we could hear his comments in our ear. As we were saying good-bye, I added a "Happy birthday, Andrew."

"Al! No!" John barked. It wasn't really a shout, but no one would mistake it for a whisper. He was quite calm later when he said he simply couldn't allow comments of that nature. The show was for viewers across Canada, not for one or two acquaintances of the participants. "There's no way we can have that," he said. "The question becomes, where do you draw the line?"

It wasn't a question of censorship, as it would have been if one of the radio *Hot Stove* people had wished a happy birthday to, say, a relative serving in the military overseas somewhere. No lives would have been endangered. But it was a reasonable policy.

With the show having been taped, it would have been easy for Shannon to chop Andrew's birthday wish from the show before it got aired. He didn't.

CHAPTER 5

Up in the Air

think I can safely say that the question I am most frequently asked is, "How did you get to be a hockey writer?" Like most of my stories, it's long and somewhat convoluted, but this is a book, not a column, so I can indulge.

In 1973, I was working for the *Windsor Star*, part of the Southam Newspapers chain. I got along well with the publisher and enjoyed working for him. When he was transferred to the *Montreal Gazette*, I applied for a job there, knowing that I could count upon him for a recommendation. He had the authority to put me on the *Gazette* staff without consulting anyone else, but he wouldn't do that, which was one of the reasons that he was good to work for. He didn't micromanage.

The managing editor, probably thinking that it was a good idea to suck up to the new publisher, decided to hire me and asked if I spoke French. I didn't. "Then you'll have to work in the sports department," he said.

That was fine with me. I had been a business writer in Windsor. Driving a new-model car around for a week, then writing a review of the experience, had its moments. But working on the sports desk in a city like Montreal seemed like a lot more fun.

I began the job under the vigilant supervision of Brodie Snyder, a stereotypical old-time newspaper deskman if there ever was one. He chain-smoked Export cigarettes (unfiltered, of course) and routinely ran up a weekly bar tab that exceeded the gross national product of a few small third-world countries.

We went through reams and reams of paper in those days. Copy boys would bring in stories by the dozen, all ripped off the huge rolls of low-grade paper that spewed out of the teletype machines. Often we received multiple copies of the same story. There would be updates to a breaking story and even if only one paragraph had been added, the entire story would be reprinted. Brodie would select the version he wanted and throw the rest into a huge garbage bin that invariably was overflowing by the end of the day.

A summer intern once dumped the remains of his dinner into that bin and was quickly informed—rather loudly and in no uncertain terms—that he had transgressed the unwritten rule. That bin was for paper only. Actually, the rule made sense. Sometimes we needed a different version of a story and having already discarded it, needed to retrieve it from the garbage. We strongly preferred a version without blobs of hoisin sauce on it. That directness was Brodie's nature. He'd tell you something once and saw no reason to ever have to repeat himself. The intern had probably been told once about the paper bin. That should have been enough.

Brodie would sit huddled over the desk, jabbing away at typed submissions, slashing and correcting with his thick pencil, and har-rumphing occasionally in disapproval. He rarely spoke, preferring instead to use an ancient Remington typewriter to pound out his messages. Or maybe it was an Underwood. The *Gazette* had both. Either way, it was ancient.

Occasionally, he would actually make a comment that didn't refer to the copy we were handling. It didn't happen often, but it was worth hearing when it came. One afternoon, Montreal was struck with tor-rential rain. Bob Morrissey, another one of the staffers, looked out the window and said, "It's really coming down out there."

"It would be a hell of a story if it was going up, Bob," grunted Brodie, still jabbing away at some copy.

Brodie's title was assistant sports editor, but really, he ran the department. The guy who was officially the sports editor did little more than write an occasional column based on the extensive research he had done in the bars on Crescent Street. It was Brodie who was in the office almost every day making all the key decisions.

I was mostly a copy editor at the time, one of the two or three anonymous souls who sat around a horseshoe-shaped desk in a small smoke-filled room, writing headlines and editing stories, acting on directions that Brodie typed out on a half sheet of what we called tea paper, which was cheap, low-grade, and probably recycled. He would slide the sheet, along with the story he had selected to be edited, across the desk.

Let me make an interjection here about smoke-filled newspaper offices in those days. When I was growing up in Windsor, one of my idols was Joe Falls, a sports columnist for the *Detroit Free Press*. Later on, I got to know Joe well and he turned out to be as good a person as he had appeared to be in his columns.

I asked him the familiar question, "Why did you get into the newspaper business?" He said he did it because it was the only one he knew where you didn't have to use an ashtray. You just threw your cigarette butts on the floor.

We had ashtrays at the *Montreal Gazette* and they were certainly used—overused in many cases. Every afternoon, Harold Atkins, another one of the copy editors, would smoke a cigar. Most of us (yes, us, I didn't quit until 1978) had at least one cigarette going. Sometimes we'd forget that we had set one on the ashtray and would light another. When I say smoke-filled, I mean smoke-filled.

One Sunday evening, the Canadiens beat writer called to complain about the way his story had been handled. Since it was Brodie himself who had been doing the handling, and not me or one of the other copy editors, this was not the best career decision ever made in the history of Canadian sports journalism. I hadn't been at the *Gazette* long but I certainly knew that a reporter calling to imply that Brodie should do a better job was not going to be well received. On this occasion, Brodie did speak—loudly and forcefully. By the time the conversation terminated, the *Gazette* was without a Canadiens beat writer.

I had covered a few Canadiens home games, but my primary duties were on the desk. Not having had anything to keep me busy while Brodie talked to the beat writer, I was waiting to continue those primary duties. Brodie briefly hammered on his typewriter. A piece of paper fluttered across the desk. "Can you go to Los Angeles with the Canadiens tomorrow morning?"

Adhering to the Brodie-imposed dogma of not talking unless it was absolutely necessary, I typed out my response and sent a piece of tea paper back across the desk: "Yes." More tea paper followed: "You'd better go home and pack. Be at the airport at 6 a.m." That's how I became a hockey beat writer.

Since my normal sleeping hours in those days were 4 a.m. to noon, that plane was leaving far too early for my liking, and I got to the airport a little bit late. Not too late, but late.

I have to backtrack a bit here. This was my first road trip with the Canadiens, but a few months earlier, I had made a short one with the MLB Montreal Expos. When baseball teams travel, they take along one or two staffers to make sure everything goes smoothly. Most flights were charters, so you didn't have to concern yourself with menial matters like tickets and boarding passes.

Furthermore, the team also provides people to handle your luggage. For the first leg of a baseball road trip, you drop off your bag in the clubhouse and pick it up in the hotel lobby in the next city. After that, you leave it in the hotel lobby on getaway day and pick it up in the next hotel lobby.

That kind of arrangement, while convenient, has its drawbacks if you're not careful. One of the *Gazette*'s baseball writers stayed out too late one night (a not uncommon occurrence) and woke up at 12:55 p.m. His luggage had to be in the lobby in five minutes so he called the desk and shouted at them to send a bellboy to his room as quickly as possible. It was a virtual emergency! Hurry!

The bellboy made it in about three minutes, during which time the writer had crammed his clothes into his suitcase, not caring whether they were folded or not, and pulled a five-dollar bill out of his wallet to make sure the bellboy didn't dawdle on his trip downstairs.

With the luggage now safely on its way, he collapsed on the bed again for a few minutes. Then he got up to get dressed. This was when it dawned on him that he had a problem. Every item of clothing he had brought on the trip was in that suitcase, and it was now on its way to the next city. And he slept in the nude.

The good news is that he was one of five Montreal baseball writers covering the team. One of them—who was also familiar with problems caused by staying out until the wee hours—went out and bought our friend some clothes. There is more good news. Not long afterwards, the *Gazette* writer swore off booze and stayed sober for the rest of his days.

This story was often recounted with great merriment when sports-writers got together and spun yarns (in pubs, of course). It rivalled the experience of another *Gazette* writer of that era who booked a flight to Williamsburg, Virginia, when he was assigned to cover the Little League World Series. When the writer reached his destination, he was a bit surprised that the airport wasn't busier, considering that such a big event was pending. That was when he found out that the Little League World Series is held in Williamsport, Pennsylvania, not Williamsburg, Virginia.

So, on my first travel assignment with the Montreal Canadiens, I was within minutes of adding my own story to this chronicle of legendary travel screwups. On that fateful morning (that very early morning, I might remind you), I learned that NHL travel was considerably more "no frills" than travel with MLB.

With no concern whatsoever for the fact that I didn't have a ticket, I wandered up to the Dorval Airport counter and asked which gate I should use for the Canadiens' charter. There was no charter. Furthermore, everyone who was supposed to be on the commercial flight that the Canadiens were using was already at the gate. With one notable exception, of course.

It appeared that my career as a hockey writer was not about to kick off with a spectacular start. In fact, if I missed the flight due to not having a ticket, I would be lucky if it didn't end on the spot. Even if I somehow managed to survive, I would be guaranteed a level of sportswriting infamy for the rest of my life.

Fortunately, my own transgression took place almost a half century ago, back when Air Canada showed a modicum of concern for its customers. The man at the counter called the gate to see if anything could be done. I was relieved. Surely the Canadiens' travelling secretary, whose job it was, among other things, to babysit sportswriters, would handle this and the matter would be quickly smoothed over. Then the guy at the gate gave me the bad news. "Hang on a minute. They're going to talk to Scotty."

I was quivering. My fate was going to be determined by Scott Bowman, known universally for his short temper and harsh demeanour. I had seen his eruptions when a player went offside during scrimmages. I knew that the players said somewhat sardonically that he had to be given credit for treating them all equally—like shit.

I wondered why they couldn't just talk to the Canadiens' travelling secretary. It turns out that they did. Apparently, Scotty Bowman was the Canadiens' travelling secretary. That's the way things were done in the NHL. After a wait that seemed interminable—probably just a minute or so—the agent started talking again. "Yes. Okay. I'll do that."

He poked a few buttons, took the boarding pass that came out of his machine, and handed it to me. "Scotty says the Canadiens will take care of it. Give me your luggage. I'll make sure it gets there on time. Go to the gate."

I remember marching briskly off into the nether regions of Dorval Airport carrying only my portable typewriter (fairly new and left over from university, not an ancient Remington or Underwood). I'm sure there was no tirade when I caught up to the team. If there had been, I would remember it. Most likely, what Scotty said was something along the lines of, "You're late, eh?"

He ended most of his sentences with "eh?" in those days. He still occasionally does today, but certainly not as often as before. Perhaps that's a result of living in the United States for so many years.

Furthermore, he does not believe in salutations. A conversation with Scotty starts as if it had just been interrupted for a moment or two. Even if you haven't seen him for a year, when your paths finally cross, his first sentence is likely to be something like, "You're living in St. Andrews now, eh?"—which is exactly what he said to me after I hadn't seen him throughout the 2004–05 lockout year and then ran into him at the Hockey Hall of Fame induction in November.

But I'll always remember that back at the start of my career, Scotty arranged an immediate ticket for a transcontinental flight for me, something that was definitely not his responsibility. And when the Air Canada bill eventually arrived at the Canadiens' corporate offices, it was probably Scotty himself who would have had to do the paperwork and arrange to bill the *Gazette* accordingly.

There were only about fifty people on the flight when it left Montreal, and the Canadiens entourage made up about forty of them. There was to be a stop in Toronto and then we would head for Los Angeles.

However, Toronto was fogged in so we were now on a nonstop. After a couple of hours, the pilot said that since there were so few passengers and the skies were so clear in that part of the world, anybody who wanted to come up to the cockpit and check out the view was welcome to do so. "And by the way," he added, "we are coming up to the Grand Canyon."

That was my first extended hockey road trip, and from a scenic point of view, because I gladly accepted the pilot's offer, it was the most memorable. There were dozens of trips after that, and in one way or another, they were usually memorable, but not for views from the cockpit. Nevertheless, I made them for the next forty years.

CHAPTER 6

Casting Call

To get a tryout in the NHL, you have to exhibit enough talent to get noticed by the people in charge. Once there, you have to prove that you belong at that level. Have a good game and you'll get back into the lineup. Have a string of good games and you'll become a regular. If you've been in the lineup for a time, you can get away with an occasional bad performance or two and be forgiven—for a while. But if you have a terrible game in the tryout stage, you'll probably never be seen again.

The premise for *Hot Stove* was pretty much the same. With a couple of exceptions, there were no guaranteed spots. To start, you were invited to take part in a show. Then, you might be invited back. If you had a few good shows, you could count on a contract for the following season—but there were no guarantees in that contract. It simply stated how much you'd be paid when you appeared. It was not until I was the senior member of the *Hot Stove* panel that I got a contract stipulating a per-show salary and a large number of appearances. There were other promises made by producers outside of my contract, but Scott Moore, who by then had somehow convinced CBC bigwigs he deserved to be running the sports department, paid no attention to them.

During the show's first few years, the job of determining who was to be on it and who wasn't fell largely to John Shannon, but only in one instance did he make the final decision without consultation.

"Every summer, before the season started, we'd get the whole staff together and go over the guys we had used last year," he explained. "We'd ask everybody who liked a guy and who didn't. Some guys got a lot of votes and some only got a few. Red Fisher didn't get any. Without exception, everybody hated Red Fisher."

But John has an affinity for tradition and for hockey's heritage. At that time, Red, who died in 2018, was the senior hockey writer in North America.

"It was one of the very rare times that I used my authority to overrule the others," John recalled. "I told them, 'He's coming back. Even if none of you guys like him, he's coming back.'

"In those days, we didn't have a studio. We just worked out of the arenas, and if the game was coming from Montreal, we would be in the Forum, and we'd probably use Red and Yvon Pedneault [a veteran Montreal French-language journalist who has worked for a string of outlets over the years]. I told Red he was probably going to be on twelve times during the season. He said that wasn't enough, and he got mad at me. All season long, every time we were in Montreal, I saw him, and even though he was on that night, he bitched at me."

That is true. I witnessed more than one of those instances. They didn't occur in private.

John continued telling me his story. "Then, when the conference finals came, everybody we'd used throughout the year was there, so I could pick anyone I wanted. I used you. Red was really pissed off at me and said I was playing favourites. I'd had enough. I said, 'Red, if it wasn't for me, you wouldn't be on at all. You're *nobody's* favourite.' He didn't talk to me for a year."

I think all of us felt that we should be on every week. It wasn't just a matter of getting your face on television; it was a matter of your status within the sportswriting community. We were all, by nature, highly competitive. We liked to break stories that no one else had even remotely suspected as possibilities. We liked the special status we enjoyed within our own newspaper because of the exposure we gave it every week on national network television. We liked to be recognized in the hockey community, not just in the dressing rooms, but at press conferences and in boardrooms, too.

And we all had egos. It's not something you brag about and there are those who see it as being a negative, perhaps even a deplorable, aspect of one's character. But the simple fact is that if you're not egotistical, if you don't think you can do the job better than anyone else, you'll never make it to the top. And in the hockey media business, *Hockey Night in Canada* was the top. So, Red wasn't really any different than the rest of us. He just didn't hide his disappointment as well.

My relationship with him followed a winding path. In my early days as a hockey writer, Red was a good friend, offering helpful insights. On my first trip to Buffalo, for instance, I went to the arena on the team bus, as was the custom, and followed the other writers up to the pressroom. In Buffalo, when you went up, you went up. It was one of the highest press boxes in the league, and I don't remember any elevators in the Buffalo Auditorium—universally known as the Aud. The pressroom was near the press box.

As game time approached, Red explained that the bizarre system used for press accreditation in Buffalo required us to go all the way downstairs and get a ticket from a press attaché. Otherwise, we wouldn't be allowed in the press box. All the other reporters had left the pressroom without making me aware of that fact. Red was like a border collie when I was starting off, herding me here and there and making my job easier.

Later on, an urban myth—often perpetuated by Red himself—built up that Red didn't talk to rookies, either players or, later in Red's career, journalists. But he certainly talked to me in my first year. I was never afraid to ask him for help, and it was always forthcoming. In many cases, it was offered before I asked.

For rookie journalists, there were a lot of important aspects to learn. For instance, some rinks offered good media meals. Some didn't. Some offered postgame beers. Some didn't. As I said, invaluable information.

But whenever we were on the road, Red was always good with useful logistical information as well: how much a cab would cost if you didn't take the team bus, and which gate to use once you got to the arena; how to access the dressing rooms after the game; and where to find the home team's coach after the game (this was an era prior to mandated coach availability).

Red wasn't much good with information regarding lively bars and clubs. I had to rely on the French reporters for that. They were French-speaking, not French, but that's the way everyone, including themselves, referred to them. Similarly, in Quebec, English speakers were generally referred to as English, even if they had never even been to England.

Red's stance of not talking to rookies started in the early seventies when Guy Lafleur joined the Canadiens. Lafleur had been touted as a generational player and he made the jump to the NHL right out of junior hockey. No rookie had received so much fanfare in Montreal since Jean Béliveau arrived on the scene.

After every game, and every practice, the French press—*Montreal Matin*, *La Presse*, *Le Journal de Montreal*, and *Le Devoir*—would swarm Lafleur and then report his day-to-day progress. Countless features were written about him as well. The *Montreal Gazette* didn't leave him alone very often, either. But references to Lafleur in the *Montreal Star*, Red's paper, were minimal at best.

This did not go unnoticed by the French media. This was, after all, the era in which Quebec separatism was in its ascension, and perceived injustices were quickly pounced upon and exposed. Red's problem was that despite being a native Montrealer, he spoke no French. And Lafleur spoke almost no English. So in order to deflect the charges of being anti-French, Red took to announcing that he didn't talk to rookies. He knew full well that after a year with the Canadiens, Lafleur's English would be good enough to deal with a reporter from an English paper. And it was. So in Lafleur's second year, Red treated him the same way the rest of the media treated him. But Red couldn't reverse his stance after that. So the idea of not talking to rookies lasted as long as Red did.

We remained friends for twenty years, but once *Hot Stove* got under way, that changed. Red saw me—accurately, as Shannon later explained—as one of the reasons that he didn't make more appearances.

He became critical of me and my work, as if it were somehow my fault that his contributions to the show weren't well received. He even started telling people that I had deserted my wife and children. Needless to say, that was not true. Red and I remained civil to each other when our paths crossed, but the relationship was chilly, to say the least.

I understood his desire to be on *Hot Stove* more frequently, but I hadn't done anything to cause him to be passed over. Others had made the decision. When Red was on the show, he tended to present himself as bitter, arrogant, and condescending, which didn't go over well with viewers. He took such a curmudgeonly approach to John Davidson on one show that JD compared him to Jack Lemmon and Walter Matthau in the film *Grumpy Old Men*. After the show, Red had the good grace to call JD and laugh about the comparison, but viewers never got to see that. What they did see was further confirmation that Red was just a grumpy old man.

Like Red, and probably many others, I once told John Shannon that I thought I should be on more often. He said, "Don't complain. I've got a drawer full of letters from Damien Cox [of the *Toronto Star*] demanding to be on the show, and you're on instead."

I never complained after that, even though Shannon admitted years later that he had exaggerated just to keep me in line. "I didn't have a drawer full of letters," he said, "but every time I saw Damien, he would plead to be on. He never was."

Eventually, even more years later, when the show had moved to Sportsnet and Scott Moore was making decisions, Cox got to be part of the second-intermission show. He quickly proved that Shannon had been right all along. The information that Cox presented was simply not of the calibre that Shannon would have demanded.

Shannon knew what interested a TV audience, and he knew that this was no longer the age of Baldy Cotton, Elmer Ferguson, and the

others from the old radio version of *Hot Stove League*. People now
demanded some variation and some insight, so he had no qualms
about arranging for a new face to appear in one of the little squares.
But it had to be someone who could be expected to tell viewers something they didn't already know. "There's nothing wrong with a little
competition," Shannon would say with a smile.

Fortunately for me, Shannon was an avid newspaper reader. When
I was at the *Globe and Mail* in the 1980s, the beat writers often had
to produce a package of notes from their sport and they became part
of a Saturday page called "The Insiders."

As far as I know, the *Globe* was the first newspaper to use "Insiders" as a label, and to require its beat writers to make public all the
little snippets that they had previously used only to entertain other
staffers over a beer or two.

John Shannon was one of the Insiders' avid readers. "The *Globe
and Mail* had the best sports page in the country in those days," he
said. "And another guy who did that sort of thing was Kevin Dupont.
He wrote in the *Boston Globe*, and every Sunday he did a hockey
notes column.

"The year before I started with *Hockey Night*, I was travelling and
picking up newspapers. There was no internet to speak of, and I would
see things like Kevin's column and I'd see the Insiders in the *Globe
and Mail*. I would marvel at this and, in many ways, be so jealous.
I'm a television guy but here were newspapers doing something that
television couldn't.

"So that was a part of the genesis of *Hot Stove*. Long before I took
over *Hockey Night*, it was always in the back of my mind that we had
to have something like that. I like to think that's what the *Hot Stove*
became for eight and a half minutes every Saturday night."

The truth of the matter is that *Globe and Mail* staffers weren't
always thrilled about being selected by an editor as one of that week's
Insiders. As I mentioned earlier, the sports staff was huge—there
were four writers just for horse racing—so for any given sport, there
was always someone else who could have been designated. Because

there was so much information in an Insiders column, a fair amount of work was required, hence the assignment's unpopularity. But I hereby forgive the *Globe* editors who selected me on a regular basis. It was because of those Insiders columns that I was given a crack at *Hot Stove* when it was still in its formative stages.

"I always read your stuff at the *Globe*, and I always loved the fact that Munson Campbell was in your back pocket," Shannon said. "Munson Campbell would tell you everything. We needed people who were hockey-centric. You had done enough radio and TV to do the job properly. You were irascible enough, edgy enough, quick enough, grimy enough to be what I wanted on *Hot Stove*."

I suppose that's all meant to be complimentary.

And while it's true that Munson Campbell, a former owner of the short-lived NHL California Seals, was what you might call indiscreet ("Geezus, Al, did you see how that guy skates? He doesn't skate, he snowshoes. It's probably because of his syphilis."), he was far from my only source. In fact, he wasn't even the best source I had at the ownership level. A certain other owner told me a lot more and would even call NHL president John Ziegler to get information for me on occasion.

I had a fax attached to my telephone answering machine in those days (younger readers will have to google that whole sentence to find out about those ancient devices). Sometimes I'd come home and find fax paper, which came in a large roll, covering the floor near the machine. My friend had just sent me a ream of supposedly confidential material that was being distributed to the NHL governors. Scrawled in the margins would be his observations and complaints.

Like most of the people who worked behind the scenes on *Hockey Night in Canada*, Shannon considered the two intermission shows to be the highlight. There was a certain amount of predictability about the games themselves, but no one ever knew what to expect in the intermissions.

Both *Coach's Corner* and *Satellite Hot Stove* were more forthcoming than anything seen on earlier versions of *Hockey Night in Canada*, and as a result, were certain to generate some strong reactions. Shannon didn't care. Or if he did, he hid it well.

"I never thought we'd ever piss anybody off because if you tell the truth you're not going to piss people off," he said. "I've never worried about that. If it's truthful then people can't complain."

The fact is, though, people did complain. On *Hot Stove*, we'd expose everything from gambling debts to DUI arrests. Over one stretch of about six weeks, we provided, on a weekly basis, the latest updates on the love triangle of Pavel Bure, Anna Kournikova, and Sergei Fedorov. Then, when we expanded it to include Pavel's father and Anna's mother, we figured it was time to let the matter slide.

People we talked about complained not because the stories weren't true but because they didn't want them made public. John stuck to his guns and told them that as long as the stories were true, he wasn't going to intercede.

"This is at a time when Saturday nights were still appointment views," he said.

Appointment views?

"Yeah. You know: I can't go out Saturday night because I've got to watch hockey. People felt that was the case, and we had a responsibility. We needed to give them a reason more than Don to keep their appointment. We needed to give them a reason more than a good game because we weren't always guaranteed a good game.

"Ralph Mellanby [a former *Hockey Night* executive producer and Shannon's mentor when he started in the business] taught me that. It was the punctuation point at the end of the week and that was what *Hockey Night* was in so many ways because if something happened on Wednesday, people thought, 'Boy I can hardly wait to see what Don says.' But Don can't cover everything. That meant we needed a catchall. We needed something to say what was going on in the other cities, something to find out what was going to happen. It was a lot more inexpensive to do the *Satellite Hot Stove* than to do more features, and there was a practicality as well. It was something I really believe in to this day.

"And there was something else. What the *Hot Stove* really was, was magic. You could be in Toronto; JD could be in Hartford; Jimmy could be in Phoenix, and you're all on the screen together. I still marvel at what television can do."

Sometimes, things were said that didn't get heard. They may have been the quick, snide comments I stuck in (a bit too often perhaps), or they may have been the beginning of points from one of the other panelists. Most of the time, John kept that under control. That squiggly little wire sticking out of our ears was there for a reason. John was on the other end and was using it to keep us in line. He might tell us which one of us should be talking or he might be urging us to move along to another subject.

When I look at some of those old shows, I can often see from my body language that I'm about to interrupt or add a point, but I don't. That would almost certainly have been the result of Shannon in my ear telling me, "Don't say anything, Al. Let him finish then we're going to break." He said "Don't say anything, Al," a lot.

Sometimes, but not often, we had two people (or more) speaking at once. John didn't mind. "That's what people do," he said. "If you're sitting in a bar and you're trying to listen to a conversation, all three or four guys are talking. Sometimes they all talk at the same time. They're all trying to get something across. It happens." Shannon wanted to break down the gap between the viewer and the viewed, to make the viewer feel part of it, hearing inside information and listening to a conversation.

Leaving us alone was all part of it. We were never scripted, and what we talked about was subject only to the whims of Ron MacLean, who gave us a lot more problems than Shannon ever did.

We'd get everybody hooked up as 3 p.m. approached, and Ron would ask JD what he wanted to talk about. JD would tell him. He'd ask me what I wanted to talk about and I'd tell him. He'd ask Jim Hughson what he wanted to talk about, and he'd say he'd follow us. So Ron would then give us a lineup. "JD, you start first with the Rangers. Jim you come in with the Canucks, then Al, you talk about the developments in Denver. Let's go."

The show would start. Ron would welcome the viewers and say, "Al, what's going on with the Los Angeles Kings?"

In one of the old shows I was watching recently, I looked at him and said, "What, you're starting with me?"

"Yes, you might as well start."

So I started. I don't remember the specifics, but I'm sure Ron, as usual, had kicked off the show by doing the opposite of what he'd said he would do.

Usually, I didn't display any reaction. It was so common for Ron to revamp the batting order without telling anyone that I was prepared for it. I just mentally shrugged it off and ad-libbed about whatever topic he raised.

Compared to Ron, Shannon was a breeze. He told us what he expected and that was it. Sometimes, during the week, he had picked up a good scoop and he gave it to one of us—usually me. But he never told us what items to use or how to present them.

"I never had a tough time handling anyone," he said. "I loved every moment of it. I never told you guys what to say. With Don [for *Coach's Corner*], it was the same way. Sometimes, if there had been a big development during the week, I'd go over to his house with a couple of black coffees and we'd sit down and talk it through. I'd say, 'What are you going to do?' and he'd tell me.

"I'd say, 'Well, that doesn't make much sense. Why don't you do it this way?' and he'd say, 'That's a better idea.' All I ever wanted from Don was for him not to embarrass himself. I wanted him to be great every Saturday.

"I'm a TV-holic. I'm a media guy—but I think as a hockey fan and a viewer first. I don't think as a player because I never played the game. But I know as a viewer what I like, so I just assume that most people like it. Most of the time they do."

CHAPTER 7

A Kathy of All Trades

J ohn Shannon was the architect of *Satellite Hot Stove*, but Kathy Broderick was the builder. As I mentioned earlier, it was during the 1994 lockout that Shannon envisioned the concept of creating a hot-news panel show to fill the second intermission of *Hockey Night in Canada*. He has no problem taking credit for making his idea a reality. However, he always quickly adds, "But Kathy Broderick put it all together."

By the time *Satellite Hot Stove* became a part of *Hockey Night in Canada*, Kathy had been in the television business long enough to be able to do any job that John could do. But John was the executive producer, and at the CBC, that meant a lot of time was required to write memos, read memos, soothe egos, explain decisions, hear complaints, attend sensitivity sessions, sit in on meetings, increase political correctness, and so on. John needed someone he could rely upon to do the jobs that he might do himself if he were able to allocate sufficient time to them.

For instance, he might have a twenty-second clip of NHL action that he wanted converted into a thirty-second promo with voice-over, intros, extros, and all the other fancy things TV people do that I don't understand.

Because Kathy was there, he didn't have to rhyme off all the requirements step by step. He could take ten seconds to tell her what was needed, even though it was a complex job. And the job would get done, just the way John wanted it.

In the interest of full disclosure, I must mention that Kathy and I have been friends for a long time. But I can assure you that however much I praise Kathy's work here, there is no evaluation that can't be fully supported. Nor is there any exaggeration.

She has been so heavily involved with *Satellite Hot Stove* that I can't leave her out, friend or not. Only Kathy and Sherali Najak were with it for every show. Even though Shannon hired her to work at *Hockey Night in Canada* after *Satellite Hot Stove* was created, he can't match her tenure. She joined the CBC in 1998, but had worked for Molstar Communications, the show's producer, before that.

For anyone who isn't familiar with the responsibilities of a producer, let's just say that everything you see on your screen sitting at home watching the game is determined by the producer. That includes camera changes, replays, crawls across the bottom of the screen, insertion of commercials, and so on.

Her job has always entailed far more than just the eight minutes of our show. After all, her official title is producer. She can and does produce games, even though she'd rather let one of the other producers handle that responsibility so she can deal with all the other last-minute problems that inevitably arise.

And during the first intermission of that game, whether Kathy was the producer or not, you might have heard Don Cherry mention her on *Coach's Corner*. Often, when Don had identified an aspect of hockey that he'd like to explore, he would use a series of clips showing examples. It was always Kathy who dug up those clips, and Don usually credited her as the source.

"I've worked with Don a long time," Kathy explained, "even before *Hot Stove* started. It became kind of my job. When you watch hockey an awful lot, as much as I did, you would know what Don needed and wanted, and we just clicked."

Don relied on her, even more than he relied on Ron MacLean. It was Ron who set him up for his observations, but it was Kathy who prepared him to make those observations and provided him with the footage to support them if necessary. They phoned each other often during the week and they always talked on Saturday morning. Then they met as soon as Don arrived at the studio in midafternoon. They would go through the material Don intended to use and if there was something Kathy didn't like she wouldn't hesitate to tell him.

"I guess with Don, it's another example of why John hired me," she explained. "I would tell him stuff. I wasn't afraid to speak up. I'm cut from the same cloth as Don and John—very loyal and trustworthy. If I thought there was something wrong, or if Don was not right about something, for sure I would tell him."

She never told me what to say on *Hot Stove*, partly because we rarely knew ourselves what we were going to say, and partly because we generally talked about things that weren't common knowledge. But she did tell me to smile more.

"Oh yeah. I had forgotten that," she said when we chatted about this book. "I did it because you always looked so mean and furious. You looked like you were about to tear a strip off somebody. You had to get that little smirk on your face so that you'd look like you were having a good time while you were doing the show."

I took that to heart and tried to smile as much as possible. You can't do it too much, but a lot more than I had been doing. Kathy was right. After that, if she was in the room while we were taping, I'd sometimes look over at her and smile, just to let her know I hadn't forgotten. And occasionally, I suppose, there was a smirk as well.

She also reminded me not to look at the monitor. Usually, there was only one camera in the room and at its base was a monitor. Believe me, it's hard not to be distracted by a live TV picture, especially one with your own face on it. But if you fall into the trap and keep looking down at it, you give the viewer the impression that you're being devious.

Even though she didn't provide a lot of direct advice, Kathy was heavily involved with *Hot Stove*. When you're dealing with four participants, sometimes in four locations, a great deal of coordination is required. That job usually fell to Kathy, and remarkably, we always managed to get everybody on the air. We almost didn't one night when JD was in Quebec City, but that wasn't Kathy's fault—or the fault of anybody at *Hockey Night in Canada* for that matter. Shannon was preparing to go without JD when everything came together at what was literally the last minute. The reality is that in the three-hour slot allocated to the first game on a Saturday night, the sixteen minutes used by the two intermission shows were far and away the most likely to provide headaches.

"There were a lot of times with satellites and feeds and with traffic and when guys were flying in or whatever, that we were really scrambling," Kathy said.

The show could be seconds away from airing and suddenly one of the remote feeds was lost. Or a prop behind one of the participants could fall. Or a light could blow. Whatever it was, it was Kathy who would immediately take over and get the show back on track. And in the early days, when the show was taped, she even had the nerve to occasionally chop some of our extraordinary insights that the world was waiting breathlessly to hear.

"Sometimes you guys didn't realize intermissions are only eighteen minutes long," she chuckled, "so with all the other stuff we had to get in, you guys could only be given about eight and a half. Sometimes you'd babble on for twelve minutes and we'd have to cut it down."

Kathy's career path at *Hockey Night* was a bit convoluted, but then, the corporate history of *Hockey Night* itself is convoluted. When Kathy was in school (what was then known as Ryerson Polytechnical Institute) during the 1990–91 NHL season, she did volunteer work as an intern with Molstar Communications. Why a company as wealthy as Molstar, a wholly owned subsidiary of Molson Breweries of Canada Ltd., couldn't pay its interns is a terrific question, but that's the way events sometimes unfold in the corporate world.

Molstar produced *Hockey Night in Canada* for the CBC and controlled the sponsorship, most of which, naturally enough, was delegated to Molson Breweries. It was a muddled situation. The cameramen and technicians were all provided by the CBC, which meant that they got their direction from CBC management. But the on-air personalities were employed by Molstar. A good production requires a great deal of cooperation between the talent and the support staff and in those days, it wasn't always forthcoming.

Even though Kathy's internship provided her with no immediate financial benefit, it paid dividends down the road. Her capabilities did not go unnoticed, so when she graduated in 1992, she was hired full-time by Molstar.

In 1998, the CBC took a brave step forward and decided that since *Hockey Night* was its most famous, most popular, and most lucrative show, it would produce it itself. The problem was that Molstar still owned some of the rights and wasn't about to give them up.

So a different version of the two-headed monster was created. Although only one executive producer is needed for any given show, *Hockey Night* had two—one from Molstar and one from the CBC. Ron Harrison was the Molstar producer and John Shannon was the CBC producer. It was still a situation fraught with difficulties, but for Kathy it represented another opportunity.

"Molstar was really a very small production company," she explained, "and because we were such a small group, I did a lot of different things for Molstar that I wouldn't have been able to do at CBC. So I was able to offer more when the CBC job opened."

I mentioned earlier that in some circles, Shannon had a reputation as a short-tempered boss who shouted at his staff. This was the era in which that reputation was established and, as is often the case with reputations, it lingered long after it ceased to be accurate.

John had to work with CBC staffers and that can test the temper of a saint. Often, when I would go to cover some sort of announcement for my newspaper job, all the Toronto-area TV outlets would be in attendance. Usually they sent two or sometimes three people.

The CBC would send eight. There was a person to do the reporting, and he had to have a guy to give him light. And that guy needed an electrician to plug in that light. And a soundman had to provide the microphone. Their driver was there as well, and with that many people, someone was needed to do the coordination. There had to be someone to keep the head office informed of progress. What the eighth person did, no one knows.

I confess I'm exaggerating a bit, but it's true that the CBC was heavily unionized in that era and always far outnumbered any other TV outlet at staged events. That was in direct contrast to the way Shannon wanted to do things, and he reacted accordingly.

As Kathy delicately put it, "The CBC people reported to John, but John was very different to what most CBC people were used to." Kathy was in the middle. She was working for John, but she wasn't working *for* John.

"I had a different relationship with John because we worked together every day but I didn't report to him," she explained. "I reported to Ron Harrison. I wasn't afraid of John, because John wasn't my boss for the first couple of years." That came later when Molstar ceded some *Hockey Night* responsibilities to the CBC.

"I think what John saw in me was the fact that I was a hard worker. I did my homework, and I did my job well, I guess." Then she laughed. "That and my no-bullshit mentality."

The two got along famously. "We are a lot alike," she said. "He was the boss, but I'm pretty intense. Business is business, and when you're at work, you're at work. That's the way I was brought up. So no matter if John blew a gasket or got upset—which didn't happen that often, actually—it didn't faze me one bit because I knew right afterwards he would say, 'Let's go for a beer. Let's go to the Madison.' It was a momentary thing. I'm not the type to hold a grudge."

If you've done game production for a while, it becomes fairly routine. But the two intermission shows, where no one knew what might happen next, always fascinated Kathy.

"I liked the fact that different personalities were on the *Hot Stove* and that was the way John designed it," she said. "Don Cherry has been a success for a very long time, and he doesn't always agree with public opinion. *Hot Stove* was a lot like that. The thing with *Hot Stove* was it was a bunch of guys from different cities with different personalities, and I think that's what made it intriguing. I liked that everyone was able to put forth their little point or whatever they had to say, and they had the floor. With *Hot Stove*, Ron MacLean would tee everybody up and everybody would have a point. People would be able to rebut, but from what I recall, there wasn't just constant chatter from everybody. There were times when people would talk over each other, but not very often. I also liked *Hot Stove* because it was always breaking news, but at the same time, if you recall, we used to tape it in the afternoon so there was always the fear that there would be something that would break in the interim."

It was a well-founded fear. On one notable occasion, which I'll relate later, it happened. And as a result there was a personnel change on *Hot Stove*. But it didn't involve Kathy. (It involved Vancouver broadcaster John McKeachie.) Kathy was a constant throughout the show's existence, from its first show to its last.

CHAPTER 8

No Mail Today

B y the time I started appearing on *Satellite Hot Stove* in 1996, I had been in the newspaper business for more than a quarter of a century. My byline had appeared countless times in the *Windsor Star*, the *Montreal Gazette*, the *Globe and Mail*, and the *Toronto Sun*. Many of the *Toronto Sun* stories were picked up and reprinted in the other *Sun* papers across the country in places like Edmonton, Ottawa, Calgary, and other cities. For a while, I had a regular column in the *Hockey News*. During the year (1979–80) that I hosted a nonsports call-in show on CFCF Radio in Montreal, I also wrote pieces for the Montreal *Sunday Express*. I had written articles for magazines like *Sport* and *Inside Sports* as well as NHL team programs in Canada and the United States. I had appeared on all the major TV networks, a number of cable networks, and a bevy of local stations across the country. But none of that—or even all of that put together—came close to matching the impact of being a regular contributor on *Hot Stove*. It was instant fame—or instant infamy.

All of a sudden, free domestic airline upgrades to business class were not unknown. In fact, they were fairly common. My significant other and I even got a free upgrade to business class on a flight to Paris because the Air Canada agent recognized me.

I didn't bother with a car while I was living in Toronto and it was not uncommon, even at nighttime, to have a cabdriver identify me by recognizing my voice. People in bars often came over to offer their opinions, and some of them (my favourite kind) sent over a drink as well.

Once, while sitting stalled in backed-up Toronto traffic in a borrowed car, waiting for some signs of movement, a driver heading painfully slowly in the other direction stopped, rolled down his window, and offered his estimation of something I'd said.

I would go into Starbucks and, after being asked to do so, give my name—Al—to the cashier. A while later, I might hear the barista say, "Your coffee's ready, Mr. Strachan." (Actually, since I promised to tell you the truth, he probably said, "Your two-percent, extra-hot-but-not-too-hot, no-foam, Colombian dark Venti Misto is ready, Mr. Strachan," but I didn't want to show how much of a pain in the ass I can be at times.)

I often got into rock concerts by showing up at the media gate and chatting briefly with the guard who knew me from my visits to that arena and from watching me on television. I saw Aerosmith, Billy Idol, the Cars, Van Halen, Styx, and many others, usually from the penalty box because the security guard knew it was a prime viewing location and arenas don't sell penalty box seats.

I got upgraded by a car rental clerk in Ottawa who told me that the eight minutes that *Satellite Hot Stove* was on the air were the only time in the week that he insisted on absolute silence from his kids.

When I was on assignment in Edmonton, I regularly stayed at a small hotel near the arena. It had only two suites, but if either one was available, I got it at regular room rate. At a much larger hotel in Vancouver, I was invariably given one of the coveted tower rooms, so high that I occasionally looked down on bald eagles gliding past. I paid the regular room rate, of course.

These reductions in price when I was working didn't affect my personal finances at all. I wasn't paying for the cars or hotels anyway. But I must admit that being accorded that kind of benefit always lifted my spirits. Eric Duhatschek, a fellow sports journalist, agreed with me when we were talking about this phenomenon one day.

"You're so right, Strach," he said. "I had a really good job at the *Calgary Herald*, and eventually I got to work at the *Globe and Mail*, and yet I always found that people paid more attention to—and talked more about—the work that I did on *Satellite Hot Stove* than anything else.

"It was particularly true all those years when I was helping coach my son Adam's hockey team. Most of those kids have no idea who you are at the start of the season, but about two or three weeks in, they'd have seen you on television and now they know that you're the guy who's on *Hockey Night in Canada* with Ron MacLean and John Davidson and Al Strachan and all of a sudden you'd be given a different level of respect.

"It was the same thing whenever you'd go out in public and it frustrated me on some levels. You think to yourself, 'I spent sixty hours a week writing for the *Calgary Herald* or sixty hours a week writing columns for the *Globe and Mail*, and all people want to talk about is this eight minutes on Saturday night'—and I might have had only two minutes of those eight.

"Don't get me wrong," he went on (as Eric is known to do). "It was a great sideline and it was terrific for my profile, but my main income and my main contributions to the hockey dialogue were in print. But even at that point, even twenty years ago, print had already been discounted in most people's minds as a communications tool. I still see myself as a print guy, even though working for the *Athletic* I'm in the online world. So the fact that people cared so much about the *Satellite Hot Stove* was, I suppose, a blessing, but also a little bit of a curse.

"You always try to be gracious about it and people were also always saying the most flattering things, but I'd often think, "Gee, read my columns, too, okay?" It showed me the power of television. During the years we were on television, I'd get recognized and people would comment on your presence. And for years after, people would still say, 'I loved you on television on Saturday night.' Some still do."

Eric had more reservations than I did about the fact that print journalism was taking a backseat to television. But we both agreed that television made us feel important—and who doesn't get pleasure out of feeling important? Furthermore, travel can be a grind, especially in a Canadian winter, but it is always made easier with a bigger room, or an upgraded car with all the bells and whistles, or a business-class airline seat.

Granted, all of this paled in comparison to the reverence that the public regularly accorded to Don Cherry. I vividly remember an occasion when we had been in Vancouver for a Saturday-night game and travelled from the hotel to the airport together the next morning. Don spent the entire limo trip singing a traditional Irish song, but since it was a typical Sunday morning, I don't remember too many of the specifics, so we'll let that pass without embellishment. I will say only that it was an intricate song with very little repetition and Don knew all the words.

When we got to the airport, we went straight to the nearest counter to pick up our boarding passes. The plan was to head for the Air Canada lounge and stay there drinking coffee until it was time to board our flight to Toronto. We marched briskly towards security and made it with only a few stoppages for Don's autograph and occasionally for mine—although the latter was usually requested as either a sympathy autograph or an afterthought once the former had been secured.

But when we had to wait for our hand baggage to clear the scanners, we were no longer a moving target, and the hordes descended on Don. He signed autographs and moved a few feet before other admirers gathered. Then he managed a small shuffle while signing more autographs and politely responding to someone whose relative had once played in the same league as Don in 1955, or someone who had a friend who had lived in Kingston sixty years ago, only a couple of miles from Don, and perhaps he knew him.

Invariably, in cases like this, people who might otherwise have gone on their way notice the excitement and come over to see what it's all about. So the crowd gets bigger. After about ten minutes of standing on the fringes of this scrum, I went to the Air Canada lounge, probably about thirty yards away, and waited for Don to show up. We still had at least an hour before our plane was to leave (Don doesn't like to cut it close), but he never did make it to the lounge. I drank my coffees alone and we finally made contact again at the gate.

That was a typical representation of what happens when Don goes out in public. Most of the time, he doesn't venture out during the day. He is imprisoned in his home, a victim of his own fame. He loves dogs and always has at least one at home. And like any good owner, he makes sure that his dog gets a good long walk on a daily basis. But in Don's case, the walk is usually in the very early morning, often before dawn, so the dog can get its exercise and not have to stand beside Don while he signs autographs, waiting to sniff the next fire hydrant (the dog, not Don).

In the evenings, Don often goes to minor midget hockey games with his son Tim, but because he's a regular in the Toronto-area arenas, and because junior hockey fans respect him, he is allowed to watch the games in relative peace.

He is so well known that when we were wandering around the streets of London, England, in 1988, he acted like an ordinary tourist and asked a passerby to take a picture of us. The man did so, and as he handed back the camera to Don, asked, "How's Blue?"

While Don was on *Hockey Night in Canada*, a clause in his contract stipulated that he must be provided with a limo to take him to and from the CBC studio on Saturdays. He does drive, but if he had to make the walk from the nearby outdoor parking lot, carrying his loud jacket of the day over his shoulder on a hanger, as he did, he'd never make it in time for the show. The situation would be similar to the one he encountered on that earlier occasion in Vancouver. He'd still be signing autographs when the players were leaving the ice after the first period. Right up to the time he was fired in November 2019, there were people who had figured out the approximate arrival time of the afternoon limo and waited for him at the studio door where he was dropped off.

So, when I say that I encountered a previously unexperienced level of fame when I became a regular on *Satellite Hot Stove*, I was certainly not in Don's league. Even so, my presence on the show brought about a benefit that is still available. I'm using it now as I write this book, for that matter.

When I lived in Toronto, I spent a lot of time hanging around a Bloor Street coffee shop. To borrow a quote from Jaromir Jagr, who was forty-three at the time and was asked if he intended to keep playing, he said, "What else would I do?"

This was the era in which I had a twenty-eight-minute workweek. On Tuesday and Thursday, I would do "Ten-Minute Misconduct" on the Score network with Steve Kouleas and one of the others, usually Steve Ludzik, Ray Scapinello, or Mark Osborne. Then on Saturday, I would do *Satellite Hot Stove* for eight minutes. That left a lot of time to settle down in coffee shops, and I gradually became acquainted with one of the other regulars, who also had a job that gave him lots of free time. This particular coffee shop was on the fringes of the University of Toronto, where the regular-in-question was a professor.

It was 2008, the time of the real estate collapse in the United States, and because financial matters were his field of expertise, we started talking about the reasons for the crash. He grabbed a paper napkin, began drawing diagrams, drew more diagrams, and showed exactly what had gone wrong and why. It was fascinating. He reduced a complex situation to an easily understood explanation—something good teachers have the ability to do. Morning after morning, we'd have our coffees together (he is even more addicted to coffee than I am) and discuss all kinds of world matters. And personal matters. In short, we became friends.

After I left Toronto, we drifted apart, but in 2015, by which time I was living in New Brunswick, one of us—I can't remember which—noticed a posting from the other on the internet. It turned out that he, too, had left Toronto and was living in Malta most of the time, although he travelled a lot.

We exchanged emails and he invited me and my partner to visit him in Malta. It's a lovely place, so lovely that I've now spent enough time there to establish resident status. A large part of this book was written during a stay of almost three months at his Maltese property, although he only joined us for a couple of weeks during that time. He still has his place in Canada and another in Italy. He merely turns over the Malta house to us and we settle in. Had I not been staying in Toronto to do *Satellite Hot Stove*, it's doubtful that we would ever have met.

It would be wrong to suggest that everyone you meet in these random encounters is a fan. But strangely enough, perhaps because it's part of the Canadian nature, people are rarely antagonistic in person.

Pretty well everyone you meet professes to like you, but they'll often concede that they have friends who hold a different view. I once golfed (I use the word loosely) with a guy who had been added to our threesome by the starter. It was around the seventeenth hole when he admitted that he had recognized me as soon as he joined the group. He finally felt emboldened enough to say something like, "You're not really a bad guy, but my wife hates you. She thinks you're the biggest asshole on television." The first part of the sentence may not be exactly right, but the second one definitely is.

I can't remember what her name was, but let's say it was Louise. By mutual agreement, I autographed our scorecard for him and added an inscription along the lines of, "To my great admirer and good friend Louise, best wishes always."

There would also be times when a group of three or four guys entering a pub might pass by our table. Most of them would stop and make some sort of pleasant comment, then point out that their friend, the one who hadn't bothered to stop but had gone on ahead, couldn't stand me.

When people have the benefit of using the internet to make a comment in relative obscurity, however, it tends to be the other way around. Now most of them want to be unpleasant, unkind, argumentative, or critical—or all of the above. And let's face it, even when an email identifies the sender, it doesn't mean much to the recipient.

There are billions of email addresses out there. Because someone uses a name that could belong to a real person doesn't really matter much. The sender can still rely on relative obscurity.

At the *Toronto Sun*, I had a full-scale battle with management over emails (around 2003). Don't forget that when *Satellite Hot Stove* started, the internet was in its infancy, nowhere near as widespread as it is now. In fact, when I suggested to the managing editor that it might not be a bad idea to modify our approach somewhat to cater to the internet, he flatly refused. The internet, he assured me, was a passing fad and the *Sun* was neither about to waste money on it nor change its ways to accommodate it.

At that time, emailing a writer to offer your comment on a story or column was a relatively new notion, but even the *Sun* realized it had to start accepting emails, if only to match the other papers, which were already doing it.

I tried responding to my emails for a little while, but wasn't particularly enthralled by the concept. Some of the people who emailed me were reacting to something I had written. But a lot of them were commenting on what I had said on *Hot Stove*.

In many cases, the emails contained a fair amount of abuse. People are much more motivated to write when they've got something to complain about rather than when they've got something to praise. And for the complainers, it seemed that it was never enough to say, "I don't think you see the situation properly and here's why . . ." It was usually something along the lines of, "You don't know what your [sic] talking about. Your [sic—they always had trouble with that word] a moron and fat and ugly and you have a stupid moustache. And your dog probably has mange and he got it from you."

The abuse didn't really bother me, although I made sure that I never passed it along to my dog. He was a border collie, which means he was very intelligent, and I'm sure his feelings would have been hurt.

Sometimes, I did try to respond to the part of the email that was marginally comprehensible, but if I did so, the correspondent assumed he (they were almost always males) had found a pen pal. He'd write back with another point he wanted to make, though usually with fewer insults this time.

One day, however, the *Toronto Sun* decreed that all sportswriters would have their email address added to the bottom of their columns or stories, thereby making it easy for readers to respond. I told them I wanted no such inclusion. Just run the column and leave it at that. But I was told it was a paper-wide edict and I should conform like everyone else.

I said that as far as I was concerned, they had four options. The first was that they could leave the email address there and I would answer the emails, but since I had a contract that spelled out pretty specifically what I had to write to earn my salary, this would be an extra duty and I would therefore bill them accordingly. Their second option was to leave the email address there and have me respond to no emails, which probably wasn't the best possible public-relations move they could make. Third, stop putting the email address at the bottom of the columns. And the fourth option would be to pay someone else to answer my emails.

Since everybody in *Sun* management tended to shrivel up and turn purple at the thought of making any extra expenditures, they ruled out options one and four. And even though public relations weren't their strongest attribute, they could see that there was not a lot of sense pursuing option two. So they settled for option three.

This was fine with me. In fact, it was what I had been asking for all along. Unfortunately, however, it tended to create something of a burden for some other guys on the staff. Still, at the *Sun*, the sports department was full of great guys (with maybe one exception), so they handled it well. And no, I'm not going to tell you who the exception was.

The abusive emailers, not people who give up easily, would send their views to guys like Lance Hornby or Mike Zeisberger or Terry Koshan, the other hockey writers, and ask them to pass along messages to me. For the most part, they politely declined, but Zeisberger told me that he took it a step further and amused himself by sending back messages saying something like, "I could do that, but I'd be wasting my time. Al doesn't care what you think."

He wasn't far off the mark. By the time I wrote something that appeared in the *Sun*, it had been researched and given a good deal of consideration. In all likelihood, I was fully aware of the existence of a different point of view, but the purpose of the column was to explain my own opinion. That's what newspaper columns are all about.

And if the email concerned something I had said on *Hot Stove*, then the email shouldn't have been sent to a *Sun* address. There's no doubt that John Shannon got letters and emails about things we had said on the show. But he fielded them himself and we never heard about it.

Whenever you're doing such a popular show, there are going to be complaints about various aspects. But correspondence disputing our facts was rare. There were charges of fabrication, of the panelists making up stories, but not the slightest evidence to back up those charges.

"I don't think in the entire time that we did *Satellite Hot Stove* that I had more than four or five complaints about you guys saying something that wasn't true," Shannon told me.

Once in a while someone is going to get something wrong. It happens. But if Shannon is telling the truth, and as far as I know he always did, that's less than one complaint a year. I can accept that.

CHAPTER 9

A Close-Run Thing

I t's no secret that over the years I was on and off *Hot Stove*. I've occasionally thought that instead of leaving quietly when someone decided that the show would "go in a different direction," I should have said, "Listen, dickhead. Without me there would be no different direction to go into. *Hockey Night in Canada* would have left the CBC in 1988 and your relatives who got you your job would never have been a part of it. You owe me the *Hot Stove* job. I'm the reason yours exists."

But I didn't. Even I am not arrogant enough to believe I was the sole reason *Hockey Night in Canada* didn't go to CTV. I'm arrogant, but not quite that arrogant. I'll give you the facts and you can decide for yourself.

In the summer of 1988, the *Hockey Night in Canada* deal between the CBC and Molstar Communications was about to expire. It was widely assumed that Molstar would continue to produce the Saturday-night games, and the CBC would provide the platform on which they would be shown. The two sides had agreed on the financial terms of a new six-year agreement but were deeply divided on some peripheral matters.

Molstar felt, with considerable justification, that their product, the highest-rated show in the nation, was a significant CBC asset. But the CBC executives treated it with total disdain and this attitude grated on Molstar. The CBC was governed by the entitled set, people who lived well off tax dollars and enjoyed guaranteed inflation-protected pensions, plush offices, luxurious travel, and numerous other perks. If they overspent their budget, they would simply tell the federal government to increase their stipend for the next year.

Their attitude towards Molstar was condescending, to say the least. These CBC bigwigs were drinkers of fine wine and spirits, not beer. If they had any interest in sport whatsoever, they wouldn't direct that interest towards a violent, low-class game like hockey. To them, *Hockey Night* was an aggravation they had to endure, something that helped keep the masses at bay and placid, not something to promote and coddle.

No wonder, then, that when Molstar's 1988 negotiators suggested to them that at various points during the week, when the CBC was filling some of its many unsold commercial spots with house ads, a few *Hockey Night* promos could be inserted, the concept was summarily rejected by the CBC.

Molstar floated another idea. It would stick a few Molson ads on the rink boards or post them over the arena entrances that would occasionally be seen during the broadcast. People watching the game would see a Molson logo, sort of like the ads that appeared in American cities. Not a chance, responded the CBC. We don't allow rink-board advertising or other random ads on our network as a matter of policy, and we're not going to change our stance for you, just because you're our biggest advertiser.

Molstar mused about modifying the show's name a bit, so that when it opened at 8 p.m., viewers would be told that they were watching *Molson Hockey Night in Canada*. The CBC decided that the Molstar representatives were funnier than anything they had seen on their sitcoms, which wasn't a very high benchmark.

The Molstar producers were nothing if not persistent. "How about when we show the midgame scoreboard that says something like 'Edmonton 8, Toronto 0' [it was the later 1980s, after all], we could put that score in a little box that has a Molson label on it?" "Think again," said the CBC.

Not long before all these discussions took place, there had been a couple of incidents in which the CBC had exercised its anti-sports clout. One occurred in 1986 and involved John Shannon, who was a CBC producer in Calgary at the time. When a game he was producing ran long and was going to force the CBC's news show, *The National*, to start a minute or two late—no more than three—Shannon kept the game on the air instead of leaving hockey fans wondering about its outcome. At the insistence of the CBC, Shannon was fired. *The National* could be delayed only with the approval of the CBC and no one there had given that approval.

As a western-based producer, Shannon wasn't widely known outside the business, so there were no serious repercussions. But then came the famous Dave Hodge incident. On the afternoon of March 14, 1987, the CBC was showing the Brier final, a curling match for the Canadian championship, between Newfoundland and British Columbia. With the score 6–5 and three rocks to throw in the final end, 6 p.m. arrived and the CBC cut away to go either to the New Democratic Party convention in Montreal or an episode of *Star Trek*, depending on where you were watching in Canada. Naturally enough, viewers, literally from coast to coast, who had watched curling for three hours wanted to see the game to its conclusion and were furious. Dave Hodge, the host of *Hockey Night in Canada* at the time, was one of those viewers.

At 8 p.m., *Hockey Night in Canada* got under way. The national game involved the Maple Leafs and finished at 10:35. In accordance with standard procedure, the Montreal Canadiens game, which hadn't finished, was joined in progress. But after regulation time, the score in that one was 3–3, so it was going to overtime. Not on the CBC it wasn't. That would require a delay to the news.

Dave Hodge was not known for keeping his opinions hidden. He had been fired as the Toronto Argos' play-by-play man in 1981 because the club felt he was "overly critical." Said Hodge, "If the Argos want more cheering in the press box, they should do more winning."

As the 11 p.m. cutoff in the Canadiens-Flyers game approached, it fell to Hodge to thank the viewers for their patronage, and to tell them that instead of now watching overtime, they would be watching the news. It was a classic moment in Canadian television. Hodge, resplendent in his robin's-egg-blue jacket, and obviously not clear about his mandate, said, "Now, er, Montreal and the Philadelphia Flyers are currently playing overtime and, er, are we able to go there or not?"

Hodge was a true professional and rarely at a loss for words. He hardly ever said, "Er." The fact that he used it on this occasion told everyone watching that he was in uncharted territory. He paused, looked around the studio for guidance, and apparently got some.

"We are not able to go there," he said with a wry smile and a shake of his head. "That's the way things go today in, er, sports and this network. And, er, the Flyers and Canadiens have us in suspense and we'll remain that way until we can find out, somehow, who won this game. Or [with a shrug] who's responsible for the way we do things here. Good night for *Hockey Night in Canada*."

At that point, he flipped his pen into the air in what was clearly an indication of his frustration and disgust at a network that twice in one day had terminated a sports telecast while the game continued. Hodge was suspended and effectively dismissed.

As far as Molstar was concerned, games should be televised to their conclusion. Furthermore, as they made clear in their early negotiations with the CBC, they thought Hodge was an excellent host. They wanted him reinstated, but the CBC wouldn't allow it. He had implied that *The National* was not sacrosanct, and such an attitude in a CBC employee could simply not be tolerated.

The stage was thus set for the entry of CTV, the privately owned network that was CBC's rival. CTV was not entering unfamiliar territory. It owned the rights to some midweek games and had been involved in a national package four years earlier, but had let it lapse because of problems caused by blackouts. It was now focused on the lucrative and higher-profile Saturday-night package, which, under the terms of the contract, had no blackout provisions.

But CTV didn't barge onto the stage at this point. It settled for hanging about in the wings and whispering loudly. Molstar was listening. Lengthy discussions were held between the two sides, but they essentially boiled down to this:

"We'll pay you the same amount of money as the CBC for *Hockey Night in Canada*," the CTV executives said to their Molstar counterparts.

"Can we call it *Molson Hockey Night in Canada*?"

"Sure. We definitely want the *Hockey Night in Canada* part for the sake of recognition and continuity, but you can add your own name if you want."

"And we had thought about rink-board ads to promote our products."

"Go for it."

"Can we put our name on the in-game scoreboard?"

"Of course you can. You're the producers. You're responsible for content."

"And can we be assured that a game, once started, will be shown to its conclusion?"

"Any other way would be monumentally stupid."

"We think we could get Dave Hodge to come back to act as host."

"That would be nice."

"Will you give us some free promotional ads during the week?"

"Absolutely. You're going to be our prime asset. Why the hell wouldn't we promote you?"

Now the deal was at CTV's fingertips. All that needed to be arranged was the inclusion in the package of a few French-language stations, and that was not expected to be a problem. The date was Monday, May 30, and industry insiders were whispering that the contract would be signed by Friday.

On Tuesday, a story I had written headed "CBC close to losing Saturday night hockey" appeared in the *Globe and Mail*. It was breaking news, known in the business as "a scoop," and considered so important by the paper's editors that they took it away from the sports section and put it on the front page.

If the CBC had any clue that CTV was planning to pirate their highest-profile show, they hid it well. The director of operations, Dave Martin, said, "I can only say (a) I know of no such thing happening, and (b) I do not expect it to happen."

In the days to come, I was assured by some that he was telling the truth and that my story had come as a complete surprise to the CBC. Others weren't as sure. They said the network had known about the CTV offer and were just waiting to react to it.

That reaction certainly came about. CBC officials immediately asked for and got a temporary reprieve from Molstar. Two months later, representatives of both sides huddled in closed-door meetings in a Muskoka resort. Among others, Dave Martin was there representing the CBC.

When the negotiators emerged, *Hockey Night in Canada* was still a CBC property—sort of. It now had a successor that was to be called *Molson Hockey Night in Canada*. It had also been agreed that the Molson name would be on rink-board ads. And a Molson tag would also appear on the in-game scoreboard. And if you were watching the CBC during the week, you might see an occasional free promo or two for *Molson Hockey Night in Canada*.

Clearly, these concessions, which had been flatly ruled out before the CTV intervention, resulted from a fear of losing a prime property to a rival network. There's no doubt that CTV was within days of doing a deal with Molstar.

Am I justified in saying that a few more days of secrecy would have made the difference, and that *Hockey Night in Canada* would have been lost to the CBC if I hadn't filed that story? Had my story in the *Globe and Mail* alerted the CBC to the impending CTV raid, or was Dave Martin lying about his lack of knowledge of the situation? Perhaps he had known about it all along and simply hoped to be able to minimize its play in the media.

Who knows? I can't say with any certainty which is the case, and I've heard assurances on both sides. Either way, it didn't guarantee me any future job security on *Hot Stove*.

CHAPTER 10

A Sharply Dressed Man

If, because you are reading this book, or for some other twisted reason that defies logic, you decide to amuse yourself by calling up old episodes of *Hot Stove* on the internet, you can probably figure out the era without hearing any volume on the clip. In the early versions, I had a full head of hair and a moustache. I also wore glasses.

But the clothing was even more of a tip-off. I always wore a sport coat—usually of the Harris tweed variety—and a garish tie. I never wore the same jacket more than twice in any season and to make sure I didn't, I would keep index cards in the jackets' inside pockets. Every time I wore a jacket, I would write the date on its card.

This tells you two things. First, my memory wasn't as good as I would like to pretend. It wasn't unusual for me to pull a jacket out of the closet thinking I hadn't worn it recently, only to consult the index card and find out that I had worn it three weeks earlier.

Secondly, I had lots of sport coats. That was one of the bonuses of travelling frequently to Boston. Our regular hotel was within walking distance of Filene's Basement—and if it's within walking distance for a sportswriter, that means it's pretty close.

Filene's was a chain of department stores, with the original emporium situated above the famous Filene's Basement. After an item in any of the Filene's stores had gone unsold for an extended period, it was marked down, sent to the basement outlet, and given a price tag that showed its date of relegation.

Once an item had been downstairs for twelve days, it was accorded a further 25 percent price reduction. After eighteen days, the discount went to 50 percent. After twenty-four days, customers got 75 percent off the list price. By that time, it was prime plunder for sportswriters. Clearly, no one else wanted it, so it was the kind of clothing that would suit a sportswriter's taste, and much more important, it was going for a song.

But why pay 75 percent of the full price? After thirty days, the items were given to charity, and if you knew where to go, you could get them even more cheaply. But no matter how much you pleaded, Filene's refused to say which charities received the items (or so I was told by a friend).

Filene's Basement provided such prime pickings for sportswriters that its location and pricing system were passed along from generation to generation. But it wasn't only the media crowd who flocked there. I saw more than one NHL general manager rummaging through the wares in Filene's Basement. When that happened, I delighted in rushing over and saying hello, just to see the look of embarrassment tinged with horror on their faces. They'd immediately drop the cheap item they were examining as if it were a hot coal. "Oh, hi, Al. How're you doing? I'm a bit lost. Do you know where the jewelry department is? I was looking for a diamond necklace for my wife."

I'm sure they'd have preferred to have me catch them visiting the Mustang Ranch in Nevada rather than Filene's Basement. Filene's not only had some excellent jackets, it usually had hundreds of great ties as well. (I'm applying sportswriters' standards here.) Look at the old clips of *Hot Stove* and you'll see me wearing ties with flowers, cartoon characters, portraits, animals, caricatures, and all kinds of tawdry artwork.

While they may not have been elegant, they gave Ron something to pun about to close the show. Although it didn't help when he occasionally mistook the art for something it wasn't, like the time he thought that my carefully selected sheep (my Scots heritage coming to the fore) were Dalmatians, and made a joke about rushing to put out fires. I suppose you could put out a fire by throwing a few sheep on it, but surely even the Scots could figure out a better way.

I have been told that since I left the hockey beat, Filene's Basement went under (weak, I know) and the building is gone. That's probably a side effect of the collapse of the newspaper business. Once newspapers cut back on travel costs and stopped sending their sportswriters to Boston, Filene's no longer had enough customers to avoid bankruptcy.

All this happened during the John Shannon era. Later, when *Hot Stove* became more corporate, we had a basic uniform. I wore the same plain black sport coat every week. No more Harris tweeds. No more Filene's 75-percent-off classics. (I never did come across the charity shops Filene's used where the jackets would have been even cheaper. Not that I went looking, of course. I just mention that in passing.)

But we were allowed to wear ties of our choice. Styles had changed so much, though, that wide, novelty ties were no longer fashionable— not even for sportswriters, so you know they must have been really past their prime.

To set the stage, I wasn't travelling by that time. I had left the *Toronto Sun* and was getting ready for full retirement. Although I had bought a house in St. Andrews, New Brunswick, I was living most of the time in Christie Blatchford's house in downtown Toronto. There's a book waiting to be written about that arrangement, too, but if I ever wrote it and told the whole truth, bookstores wouldn't know what to do with it. Even though, by definition, it would be nonfiction, it would deserve to be placed in their postapocalyptic fantasy section.

I presume you know who Christie Blatchford was. Let's just say that she was one of the greatest newspaper columnists that Canada has ever produced, and her 2008 book, *Fifteen Days*, won the Governor General's award as the best nonfiction book of the year. Not many people can read that book without dabbing their eyes a few times.

She died while this book was being written—in February 2020— after a battle with cancer. It came as a shock to those of us who knew her. The consensus was that no matter what an insidious foe cancer might be, it would be no match for Blatch.

We were all very familiar with the type of vocabulary that Blatch always used, and when it became known that she was battling cancer, more than one person said, "She'll just tell the cancer to fuck off."

She did beat the cancer in her hip by having the hip replaced. And the cancer in her lower back succumbed to radiation treatment. But the tumor in her lung proved to be more than she, or the chemotherapy, could handle. She hadn't smoked for many years—probably twenty—but cancer is invasive and once in her body, moved into her lung.

She knew, during her illness, that I was writing this book and she knew the approach that I would take in describing our relationship. "Of course," she said. After she died, I thought of rewriting the parts that pertain to her. I often find myself thinking about when a survivor insists that the deceased would have wanted that person to play a game, or perform in a show, or tell a few jokes. I wonder whether that's the truth or just a rationalization. But just before Blatch went into a hospice, we were talking on the phone and the conversation was winding down. I told her she had to pull through and that we had had a lot of laughs together.

"Don't go getting fucking maudlin on me," she said. That was the last thing of consequence she ever said to me. After that, it was just the usual windup to a phone conversation. So I think I'm safe in saying that the anecdotes about her in this book can be used in the same way that they would have been used if she were still alive. But I do miss her and it tore me up when she died (if that's not too maudlin).

I always felt that when I was living at Blatch's I was part of her menagerie—and not the most important part. She had two—or sometimes three—cats, a dog, and occasionally another dog or two that she had agreed to watch for a friend.

But she had only one couch in the living room and one chair, which the dog liked. One day, she decreed that we had to watch an episode of *The Wire*, so I scooted to the chair before the dog could get there.

"There! Now you've hurt the dog's feelings!"

"How could I hurt that dog's feelings? He's dumb as a post. You should have got a pet rock. It would have been smarter and wouldn't have chewed your gear shift and turn signal like he did."

"That's his fucking chair. You sat in it. Now his feelings are hurt. Look at him."

"I'd rather not. He's as ugly as he is stupid."

"Get the fuck out of his chair!"

"Fuck off! I'm staying here. I'd move for a border collie. Not for him. Anyway, I thought you were pissed off at him for eating your purse."

"That was your fault, not his. You should have been keeping an eye on him."

And so it went. Another random moment chez Blatchford. Oddly enough, neither one of us got upset at this sort of dialogue. By virtue of her job, which required her to sit quietly in courtrooms and watch injustices unfold, she occasionally (some might say often) needed to blow off some steam. For my part, I held the opinion that she also needed someone to stand up to her once in a while because she had a well-deserved reputation as someone who terrorizes editors.

But our relationship also had a much more pleasant side. We would often go out for a quiet dinner at one of the better restaurants near her house. On occasions like that, it was as if we were siblings, relaxing together, absorbing the ambience, and sharing our hopes and confidences over a fine meal and a bottle of wine.

In 2010, after I left *Hot Stove*, she wrote a column in the *Globe and Mail*. This is an edited part of it.

My friend Tracy always said that the sportswriter Al Strachan was the best husband I never had.

We didn't have that kind of relationship, which is just as well, since our battles were bloody enough without the added ammunition intimacy bestows. During the year and change that he lived in my house as a freeloading roomie, we were often at one another's throats first thing, which, given Strach's hours and general indolence, tended to be about noon.

The sleep barely out of his beady blue eyes, he would make some supremely confident, dead-wrong, idiotic pronouncement about some subject about which he knew bugger all, usually a subject I was writing about, and my head would explode. Then we'd go at it hammer and tong for a while, until he got bored or I realized that, like Lucy with the football, once more I had been his Charlie Brown.

Anyone watching us would have assumed we'd been married for decades and were staying together purely for the sport of it.

Strach moved back to St. Andrews, N.B., when he was fired from Hockey Night in Canada just before Thanksgiving last year.

(Well, in fairness, he sort of moved out. As is his habit, he left behind an assortment of sports bags he acquired for free and a truly revolting collection of short-sleeved shirts in astonishing colours of mint green, beige, pale brown, dark beige and light blue, so well-worn they are almost translucent, and the suit he bought at Honest Ed's, on sale, for as I recall it, $12.99. He used to wear this on Hockey Night, sitting beside fellow commentators wearing $3,000 suits. I hate to admit it, because I believe deeply in always paying more than you should, but he looked as good as they did. From a distance.)

Blatch lived right downtown—in the Spadina-College area for those who know the city. Every Saturday morning, while she was out torturing herself by running through inclement weather with a bunch of equally maladjusted friends, I would head over to a nearby coffee shop for the usual morning sustenance (a muffin and six coffees), then troop over to Honest Ed's at Bloor and Bathurst. Honest Ed's had an incredible assortment of tacky merchandise (my personal favourites were the life-sized plaster busts of Elvis Presley), but more important, it had rack after rack of cheap ties.

Each Saturday morning, I would peruse the Honest Ed's tie selections and pick one that was sufficiently innocuous to wear on *Hot Stove*. For the most part, they were ties that wouldn't look out of place at a funeral. (No comments about the countenances of some *Hot Stove* panelists, please.) Like Filene's, Honest Ed's is now gone, too. Maybe there's a message there about catering to the clothing taste of sportswriters.

With a couple of hours to kill before it was time to head to the studio, I'd go home and listen to Blatch complain about shin splints, knee pains, blisters, frostbite, and all the other afflictions that are part of the fun of jogging along Toronto sidewalks in the winter slush. I always managed to be at the CBC studio before 3 p.m. Coincidentally, that's the time the free meal was served.

With the first game being televised at 7 p.m., action around the studio started heating up around four. With games in three or four cities on the horizon, most of the staff would be busy with all the coordination that was required and wouldn't get a chance to eat after that time. So the meal, a full catered buffet-style dinner with numerous choices of main courses, was served at 3 p.m. In order to further the sense of camaraderie between *Hot Stove* and the rest of the crew, I'd join all the others for dinner. I know my priorities.

Once everyone else returned to their jobs, my real work began. I'd wander down the hall to the makeup room, where Lianne Harrower would share a bit of CBC gossip while valiantly using everything short of sandpaper in her attempt to tone down the glare off the top of my head. Once she had finished, I would head upstairs to the fifth floor. The studio was on the tenth floor.

I remind you that this was my usual course of action during the later stages of *Hot Stove*, around 2008–2009. In the show's earlier incarnation, when I was travelling a lot, the work of gathering information had been done during the week because I encountered hockey people on a regular basis. But now that I wasn't travelling, I had to get on the phone and start dredging up items for the show.

Sherali Najak was the executive producer, and as such, he had a big office with lots of phone lines. For up to three hours every Saturday, while he was busy in the studio, I would sit in his office and get on those phones to prepare for the show. Usually, it didn't take three hours. At some point, the other guys on that night's panel would arrive. Apparently, unlike me, they didn't recognize the importance of maintaining the *Hot Stove* camaraderie by getting involved with the 3 p.m. meal.

Around six o'clock, we would share whatever insights we were planning to use. At that point, more phone calls were sometimes required. As you might expect, we all had good sources, but we didn't all have the same good sources. If we could help each other by making more phone calls to supplement the information we already had, we always did it.

I can honestly say that not once during my time on the show did I ever encounter any pettiness, jealousy, or selfishness when it came to preparing a story. If any panelist could help another panelist by getting a bit more information, it always happened. There were even instances of a "rumour" being shelved because someone unearthed information that cast doubt on its accuracy. We were a true team. The product was always at the forefront.

That attitude began when John Shannon created the show and it prevailed throughout. Shannon himself would often hear a juicy bit of information, and he would pass it along for us to use on the show—without any attribution, of course.

About 6:30, we'd let Ron know what we had and which item should get primary billing. If Scott Morrison was on the panel that day, he would be the one to take it to Ron. Otherwise, we'd call Sherali Najak, and he would pass it along. We all knew, of course, that the item we had flagged as the most important would probably be the one Ron would raise last—if at all.

We would usually stay in Sherali's office to watch the game, but not always. At one point, it had been my custom to watch the game in the little room allocated to Ron and Don. It had comfortable furniture, a coffee table, a place for Don to hang his jacket of the day, and a few monitors. It was also bugged, so that the producer would know what direction *Coach's Corner* might take. But there was no secret about it. It was just another form of internal communication.

Furthermore, Ron wore a cordless microphone from the moment he arrived in the early afternoon, and as a result, Sherali was able to hear every word he said at any time—either in the bugged room or through Ron's microphone if he was wandering around the cavernous studio, which he often did. This meant that because Don was usually in the same room or in Ron's company, Sherali could hear almost every conversation in which Don got involved.

Some of those conversations were with me. Don and I are close friends, and that friendship goes back to 1974, when I was at the *Montreal Gazette*. We share an interest in British naval history and over the years, we often talked about it. Don badly wanted to spend some time in England with someone who shared that interest, knew his way around the appropriate locales, and could take him to places connected with the man he ranks as his "first star of history," Lord Horatio Nelson. So in 1988, we spent a week in London. Don's first wife, Rose, a lovely lady, was still alive at that time and when he returned from London, Don, in his usual frank fashion, told Rose that he truly loved her and that even though they had enjoyed a wonderful honeymoon, he had just finished the best week of his life. It was therefore natural that I would chat with Don on the set, either in the afternoon while waiting for the meal or while watching the first period of the game in his room.

It might have been natural, but it wasn't to Sherali's liking. If you're the executive producer of *Hockey Night in Canada*, one of your top-level priorities was to prevent Don from going too far. So when Don and I got together and talked about politics, as old friends do, it sometimes, in Sherali's view, got Don worked up. And a worked-up Don was liable to take those volatile emotions onto *Coach's Corner*.

So Sherali issued an edict: I was banned from talking to Don until his segment had ended. As a result, even though there was a time when I used to watch the first two periods of the game with Don, I eventually had to watch the first period upstairs in Sherali's office.

"Nobody should be talking to Don during the first period," said Sherali, "especially you. He just needs to be in his own thoughts and focus on what he was going to say in the first intermission. That's the ultimate autonomy—not being influenced by anybody. Sometimes that autonomy comes through loneliness—being alone, thinking about what you actually think.

"Don is always so nice," Sherali continued. "He'll sign anything. He'll talk to anybody. I felt pressure when people talked to him because I just wanted him to be ready to go on the air."

Wherever the *Hot Stove* panel went to watch the second period, we would all gather on the set with about five minutes left on the game clock. Lianne would come over to once again fight overwhelming odds and try to make us look presentable. The floor manager, David Sealey, would add his contributions to the cause.

David was as good a floor manager as there is. No tiny piece of fluff on a jacket escaped his attention. Any slightly crooked tie was straightened. If we were in early November, he would dig into his poppy supply and put one on our jackets—always perfectly centred on the lapel. Our chairs were always equidistant from each other.

He'd tell us when it was time to get ready. At that point, being the ranking veteran of the show, I'd often try to take the edge off a bit and say something like, "Let's have a good one, guys." I think maybe I watched *Hill Street Blues* too often.

Sealey would say, "Four. Three . . ." Next came two fingers. The time for talking had passed. Then one finger. And we were on.

After our show had finished, we'd watch all of the third period, sometimes together, sometimes not. Morrison and I liked to scoot over to what was then the Air Canada Centre and watch it live. Sometimes we'd watch it in the room with Don and Ron. But whatever we did, we would always go for a drink after the game.

And that brings us back—finally—to the subject of clothing. We were invariably recognized in those days. Merely by looking around, you could always tell the people who had recognized you. They would glance over often, but even if they didn't, there was something about their look that made it clear they knew who you were, but, for the time being, at least, weren't going to introduce themselves.

The people who had been in the bar for a few hours had probably seen the show, but whatever the case, we were generally asked for an autograph. At that point, I'd autograph my tie and give it away. People seemed to like this idea and it worked for me. I wasn't going to use it again and anyway, Honest Ed's had lots more.

CHAPTER 11

One of Ours

In newspaper sports journalism, you are part of a team—nominally, at least. During most of the *Hot Stove* years, the panelists tended to work for large newspapers that sent more than one staffer to major events, such as the Olympics, Super Bowls, or Stanley Cup Final. We knew very well what teamwork was. We covered professional sports teams for a living.

But we weren't always very good at teamwork ourselves. On one occasion, the paper I was working for sent its basketball writer and a columnist to cover an NBA playoff game. On the flight home, the columnist slapped the writer, a man truly devoted to basketball. The columnist got suspended for a couple of weeks, but the writer quit in disgust at what he considered to be a punishment that was too lenient. Ironically, the columnist returned to work to cover the NBA Finals, while the writer, now at the bottom of the hierarchy at his new paper, stayed at home.

Usually discord didn't get that physical, but it was definitely common. Turf wars and backbiting were all part of the game. The *Toronto Star* once had two high-profile writers who wouldn't talk to each other. I vividly remember an Edmonton Oilers playoff game in which they were assigned adjacent seats in the press box. So that their approach didn't overlap, each had to find out the tack the other was taking. But rather than speak to each other, they phoned the office in Toronto to ask what angle their colleague intended to use.

On *Hot Stove*, we were much more of a genuine team, and that approach changed Eric Duhatschek's life. He was living in Calgary and covering hockey for the *Calgary Herald* when he became a fairly regular contributor to *Hot Stove*. He wasn't on every week, but he was on frequently and deserved to be. He worked hard to make sure he did a good job.

"It took a while," he said. "But I found that over time, I got fairly comfortable with the format. In the beginning I was extremely nervous. I'd tape the shows and go back and watch them, and I would see the palpable nervousness that I was displaying. It was such a great platform."

In 1999, the *Herald* went on strike and John Shannon, who always saw the *Hot Stove* participants as a team, decided to step in and help Eric's cause by using him more often.

"Eric was one of ours, and it was putting food on his table," he explained, "so we kept using him. I think we had him on eight weeks in a row."

"I was eternally grateful," said Eric. "He went out of his way to help me out. Even though that was an extremely difficult time of my life, I still remember, and am grateful for, the help that John and other members of the hockey community gave me. Steve Dryden, the editor of the *Hockey News*, was another guy who sent extra work my way in that period."

But Shannon also had to deal with those who were less charitable to Eric.

"At some point in there," he recalled, "the *Calgary Herald* phoned and said, 'We're on strike and we have another guy you can use instead of using Eric all the time. We'd like you to use him.' I said, 'We never identify Eric as being from the *Calgary Herald* because he's not working there right now. As you say, you're on strike. We'll keep on using him.'"

Eric remembers the incident vividly. In those days, the guys not in the home studio had very little time to talk to the producer before the show began. The connections would be made, we would all confirm that we could hear each other, and we would quickly spew out our list of potential discussion subjects. But on what turned out to be a memorable day for Eric, the Calgary set had been in use before *Hot Stove*, so it was taking a little longer to get the hookups finalized. He had a chance to talk to Shannon, who was waiting patiently in Toronto.

"I got an interesting call today from the *Herald*," Shannon told him, and then said that they wanted one of their people to replace him. "They didn't use the term 'scab,' but essentially they were offering Larry Tucker because when we were on strike, Tucker was there as one of the so-called 'replacement workers.' They brought him in to write sports."

Tucker had been a sports columnist at the *Calgary Sun*, so he wasn't inexperienced, but he was completely out of the newspaper business when the *Herald* brought him in while their staff was on strike.

Eric continued. "So I'm about to go on the air live and Shannon tells me this story and probably, it was the wrong time to tell me. I'm thinking to myself, 'This is how low those people have sunk. I've got two young kids. Their mom is a stay-at-home mom, and I'm out walking on a picket line. *Hockey Night* is the one source of income I've got during this strike to feed my young family and they are trying to take it away from me.' This is the honest-to-God truth. Up to that point in the strike, I hadn't decided what would happen afterwards because I didn't think it was going to last too long. That moment that John told that story, I decided I would never go back to work for the *Herald* again, because if they are the kind of people that would do this to a person in distress, then I don't want to work for them anymore.

"When the strike did eventually end—after eight months—they came to me to talk about going back, and I told them I would not work for them anymore. They were really surprised. I was thinking, 'Are you kidding? You tried to take away money that I was earning legitimately when I'm under intense financial pressures.' It was appalling to me that people could behave that badly.

"So there I am, live on the air, and I'm not thinking about the show. I am thinking, 'What a bunch of fucking assholes.' I was just shaken by this news. In my head, I resigned from the *Calgary Herald* at that moment. I stayed on the picket line for another six months, then I took my package and went to work for the *Globe and Mail*, which was a great career move."

Had it not been for *Hot Stove*, Eric might have stayed at the *Herald* until they started doling out golden handshakes, not unlike almost every other paper in North America. Even so, despite Eric's distress, if you had watched that edition of *Hot Stove*, you would not have noticed any flaws in his performance. He is a true professional. I don't know anyone in the business who works as hard and is such a perfectionist. And believe me, I know him well.

We all did a lot of work to make sure the show had some real meat to it, but I think Eric was the hardest worker. We all had plenty of items to discuss, but when the show was over and we got together to talk about what we'd done, it always seemed that Eric had more leftovers than the rest of us.

From 1988 to 1994, I lived in Calgary working out of the *Globe and Mail's* bureau there, and during that time Eric and I became more than newspaper colleagues. We were great friends. I rarely missed a Flames game when I was in town, and I always sat beside Eric in the Saddledome press box. Somewhere along the way, it became my responsibility to provide a bag of popcorn. The stuff in the concessions was a close cousin to Styrofoam, but I lived near a popcorn store that offered a number of delicious flavours. I would vary my choices, but sweet-and-sour ranch probably topped the list.

So there we would sit, keeping an eye on the game, confident in the knowledge that if we missed something, the monitor above our head would show a few replays of it. In the meantime, we were mostly filling our faces with popcorn and talking about our hockey pools.

Eric and I were in a lot of hockey pools. I mean a lot. I remember one game when Danton Cole scored for Winnipeg. We began to discuss the pool impact as we usually did after any goal. I said, "You know, Eric, I hate to say this but I think Danton Cole is the only guy in the NHL we don't have in some pool somewhere." It was a stretch, of course, but because of the strange rules of some of these pools, there weren't many players who weren't on at least one of our lists.

By virtue of the nature of our jobs, we were often able to spend a day skiing—as long as it was a game day. I lived in the southeast of Calgary and would call Eric when I was about to leave home. He lived in the northwest and by the time I got to his place, he had brewed a thermos of coffee, which would get us through the trip to Lake Louise or Kananaskis. It got dark around 3 p.m., so we had plenty of time after a day on the slopes to drive home, shower, change, and get to the Flames game. We hung out together when we were on the road. Our whole families got together sometimes when we were at home.

The point is, we were close. And as you might expect, there was a lot of hockey talk. I think we both educated each other and had a lot of fun in the process. (Although my elder son, Andrew, who joined us on some of the skiing trips, says his definition of hell is being in the backseat while Eric and I sang along with Don McLean when "American Pie" was playing.) Eric and I are still good friends—still in hockey pools together, but nowhere near as many—and like most old men, which we are now, we reminisce a bit about those days, and the subject of *Hot Stove* often arises.

"I wish we'd got more stuff right," Eric said not long ago. "One time we had Eric Lindros going to a team he did not get traded to, but I think that our track record was pretty good in terms of getting things right, so I don't regret anything I ever said.

"I remember one time Murray Edwards called after the show. He was one of the Flames owners, and he was mad about something I'd said and he called me at home. I can't remember what it was that I'd said, but he was fuming. He wasn't saying we were wrong; he was just mad that we'd mentioned something he didn't want discussed. So I talked him off the ledge and that was that, and then I said to him, 'By the way, Murray, don't call me at home on a Saturday night.'"

Saturday night calls to *Hot Stove* panelists were not unfamiliar.

In the latter part of his career, after he had done a stint in a drug rehabilitation clinic, Theoren Fleury was playing for the New York Rangers. During the week, there had been some fuss in the media about Fleury having been seen in a bar.

I checked out the story and found that he had done nothing wrong. I felt it was important to let people know that Fleury was still living a clean life, no matter where he might spend his evenings. There was never any hard script on our show, so I was searching for the next sentence while finishing the first, and it popped into my mind that he could even visit a cultural spot if he wanted. He could go to the theatre or the opera or a ballet, for instance. For whatever reason, I chose ballet. So that's what I said.

I was on my way home in a cab when my phone rang. It was John Rosasco, the Rangers' PR man, telling me that Glen Sather, the general manager, was angry and wanted me to call him right away. It turned out that Sather was furious because I had said that Fleury had gone to a strip bar. In NHL jargon, "the ballet" always refers to the Chez Paree strip bar in Montreal.

"Did you see the show?" I asked Sather. He hadn't. But someone, obviously a hockey person, had passed along the word, having drawn the conclusion that I was referring to a cultural activity somewhat less refined than a performance by the Bolshoi Ballet. Sather and I were good friends, so we were able to chuckle about it, and for once, no real harm had been done.

Some stories pan out. Some don't. Eric had one of the former that topped his list. "The biggest story I ever broke on *Satellite Hot Stove* was Ray Bourque to Colorado," he recalled. "It was the segment before the trade deadline and most of the talk was that Ray was going to Philadelphia. It was one of those cases where you got information accidentally sometimes. We've all had those. Sometimes you're talking to someone about Player X and Player Y and you get what you need. Then you're just shooting the shit afterwards and he says something off the cuff. I was talking to some general manager and he said, 'Will you guys be talking about Ray Bourque on your show?'

"I said, 'Yeah. We will.'

"He said, 'Have you mentioned Colorado?'

"I perked up. I said, 'Why? Do you think Colorado is in on it?'

"He said, 'Oh yeah. [Colorado GM Pierre] Lacroix is in on it. Don't sleep on Colorado.'

"I think he only said it because he wanted to give me a little shot. He said, 'Remember last year when Colorado traded for Theo Fleury and you guys didn't have it?'

"I did. I hadn't forgotten. I knew Theo well, but we didn't have that. So when the other guys on the show were talking about Bourque and the other teams were mentioned, I said, 'Don't sleep on Colorado. Remember last year when everyone was trying to figure where Fleury was going to go, and at the last minute, Lacroix pounced? That's the way he works.' A day or two later, it happened."

But just because you were right, and had broken some news on the show, didn't mean that MacLean considered it worthy of subsequent promotion. We always felt that at *Hot Stove*, we were treated like the bastard son of *Coach's Corner*. It wasn't Don Cherry's doing and he never caused us the slightest aggravation, but we felt that his segment was given preferential treatment. When Don gave Ron a list of things he wanted to talk about, that's what they talked about. Many of us felt that Ron did not treat *Hot Stove* with the same reverence.

Kathy Broderick also dredged through files to provide Don with any clips that he might need to either support his views or confirm the accuracy of his earlier predictions. We weren't really upset about it, but being sportswriters, we always liked to whine a bit, and management's catering to *Coach's Corner* was a readily available topic.

"If Don Cherry would have said that Bourque was going to Colorado, they would have grabbed that clip and shown it," Eric continued. "So the next week I decided to drop a hint. We're getting ready for the show and I said, 'Ron, did you notice that Ray Bourque got traded to Colorado like I said?' He said, 'Oh, that's right. You did have that.'

"And I'm thinking, 'Fuck me! That was the biggest scoop in hockey last week and we had it and they had completely forgotten about it. They don't know this? I have to remind them that five days earlier, that the biggest story at the time had come from *Satellite Hot Stove*?'"

We always felt that Ron's favourite part of the evening was being with Don. They were like a coupled entry at the racetrack. They could have worn bibs showing 1 and 1A. People talked about "Don and Ron." But nobody talked about "Ron and the *Satellite Hot Stove* crew." With Don, he was part of the show and could throw in some arguments. But John Shannon repeatedly made it clear to him that on *Hot Stove* he was a traffic cop. Just direct the flow, he was told. Don't drive your own car.

"I don't think he liked being the traffic cop," suggested Eric. "I think he also felt that he had something to contribute to the conversation. I think that there was always a push-pull in his own mind—that in theory, he should just be directing traffic, but I think he also wanted to get into it.

"I remember a lot of times where JD and I would be on one side of an issue, especially on something about officiating, and you'd be on the other side and Ron would join you. That didn't bother me because two against two is a fair fight but I don't think that should ever be the intention of the host. The host should move it from you to me to JD and back and forth."

Eric was also unable to resist complaining about the one constant when dealing with Ron. "The thing that I found frustrating about Ron sometimes was that you would spend all day preparing for *Hot Stove* and talking to general managers and such, then something would occur to Ron just before we went on the air and he would say, for instance, 'I know we're going to start with the Theo Fleury trade rumours, but let's talk about this.'

"Then we would talk about something we hadn't even thought about preparing for, and it would be off the cuff. Time would be spent on it. Ron wanted everyone to make a point. Now you'd find yourself coming to the end of the eight minutes and you'd be thinking to yourself, 'Wow, I did all that research and we didn't get to half of it.' That was a source of frustration to me sometimes because I spent a lot of time preparing for that segment. That's how I spent my Saturdays."

I agreed and tossed in my usual facetious observation. "Well, don't complain. He'd give you three seconds at the end."

"That's exactly what he would do," fumed Eric. "We're into the countdown and he'd say, 'Wasn't there something you wanted to say about so-and-so?'

"And I'd say, 'Yeah, he's going to be traded to Philadelphia tomorrow.' Which had been my main item. I would always console myself by thinking the cheque is in the mail and if they're happy, I'm happy."

That was the approach you had to take. One of the things every *Hot Stove* panelist learned over the years was that Ron MacLean ran the show the way he wanted to run it. He had his own ideas regarding the value of a story and he was in a position to make sure that the structure of the show would conform to those ideas, not the ideas of the panelists.

CHAPTER 12

The Greatest Years

I sometimes wonder if our show would have been as successful as it was if we'd had someone other than John Davidson in the token American role. JD isn't an American, of course. He was born in Ottawa and grew up in Western Canada. He was in every sense, as Don Cherry would say, "a good Canadian boy." But in John Shannon's vision of presenting a continent-wide scope for *Hot Stove*, JD was tagged as the representative of the United States, and he did the job in superb fashion.

The two had a TV history together. Before he started doing colour on the New York Rangers' telecasts, JD had worked on the *Hockey Night in Canada* games from Alberta. Shannon was the producer, and although their careers had diverged, Shannon saw *Hot Stove* as a perfect vehicle for his old buddy. So, almost every week, if John Shannon was the producer, JD was one of the panelists.

Unlike the rest of us, JD had had a solid hockey career in his past. He was a highly touted junior goaltender and eligible to be drafted in 1973, in the midst of the period when the Boston Bruins and Montreal Canadiens were NHL powerhouses. The Canadiens were more of a powerhouse, but many hockey people suspected that the big difference between the two teams was the goaltending. The Canadiens had plenty. The Bruins didn't. It was a different era. It was a time when the Stanley Cup was awarded in April and the amateur draft was held in May. Furthermore, goalies were never drafted high in the first round.

However, it was an open secret the Bruins would use their pick—sixth overall—to select Davidson. It was also anticipated that he would be the first goalie in NHL history to make the jump directly from junior hockey to the NHL. And, as it turned out, he was.

But the Bruins' best-laid plans hit a bit of a roadblock along the way. The Canadiens' legendary general manager, Sam Pollock, had traded his way up to fifth pick in the draft. He didn't need another goalie, even one of JD's calibre. He had Ken Dryden. But he certainly didn't want Davidson to wind up in Boston. So he traded his No. 5 draft pick to the St. Louis Blues, another team in need of a goalie. Sam was never one to brag publicly. In fact, he said very little publicly. But in private, he explained his philosophy regarding opponents, especially threatening opponents such as Boston: "It's just as important to fuck them in May as it is to fuck them in April."

So JD went to St. Louis before the Bruins could get to him, and the Canadiens kept winning Stanley Cups, significantly aided in that regard by the contributions of the guy they drafted with the St. Louis pick that Pollock got in the deal. That was Bob Gainey.

I mention all this to justify the tremendous respect we all had for John Davidson. He had been a genuine NHL star, playing first in St. Louis, then in New York with the Rangers. He was a hockey lifer and when his career was over, he had to start replacing the body parts that the game had taken away from him—both knees, for instance.

In a remarkably foolish move (his assessment, not mine), he got them both replaced at once. Let's just say that it's a good thing he has a high pain threshold. And he strongly urges anyone needing new knees not to do what he did. Somehow, though, during the recuperation period, when he was on the show and could hardly walk, he was always cheery. In fact, I've never known him not to be cheery, no matter what the circumstances might be.

JD says he was enjoying himself. "*Hot Stove* was fun, boy," he recalled. "Those were some of the greatest years of my life. On Saturdays in the afternoon, I'd drive to the White Plains railway station, take a train to Grand Central. I'd walk about four or five blocks, go up to the thirty-fourth floor or whatever it was, and they'd hook me up and we'd do the *Hot Stove*. It was outstanding. You'd talk a bit before you went on and give all your stuff to Ron MacLean. He'd do the old bob-and-weave and get everybody involved."

Like the rest of us, JD got irked when MacLean instituted his own agenda after we'd agreed on a totally different approach.

"That was probably the one negative about the whole thing," Davidson said. "Sometimes you'd leave and you hadn't got all your stuff in because of time restraints. The show ended and you had got some things in, but not what you really wanted to get in. You couldn't hold it over. By the time next week came around it was old news.

"But I'd get a lot in, so I'd leave, walk back to Grand Central, take the train back to White Plains, and be home. It was great. I really enjoyed those Saturdays.

"That was when the Rangers weren't playing. If they were playing, I'd go to Madison Square Garden after we taped. Sometimes the Rangers were on the road so we'd do it somewhere else. But it always worked. It was amazing how the television world changed at that time. There were satellites and remote hookups. That's when all that stuff was being born. So it's like John Shannon says, 'We changed the world,' yeah."

JD and I took a somewhat different approach to the proceedings, but that was all part of the format. He would invariably support the league's stance in a controversy, but I wouldn't. More likely, I had started the controversy. But we both had the same goal. We wanted to make the NHL better.

My style was to be abrasive and prod the hockey establishment into working harder to overcome the weaknesses. JD preferred to be more patient (or reasonable) and say that the league recognized the problems and was working on ways to deal with them. And he could usually be specific about the actions the league was taking.

I used to tease him about being a mouthpiece for NHL commissioner Gary Bettman. He wasn't. But the two were on good terms, and because Davidson lived in New York, he was expected to provide the view of the league's New York head office, which he did.

"The only thing I found hard about doing *Hot Stove*—but I enjoyed it—was trying to find different stuff to talk about every week," JD said. "I wanted to get stuff that wasn't mundane. I tried hard. I felt that if people were going to watch it, you might as well make it interesting for them. So yes, I would talk to Gary [Bettman] once in a while. The one approach I always took was: Why would we try to kill hockey? To my mind, it's the greatest game in the world. Sure, we can always make it better. There's no doubt about that. And a lot of these discussions were worth having, but I would never get down on the game and kick the shit out of it. For what reason?"

To my mind, he's absolutely right. If you don't like hockey, don't watch. Go watch whatever sport you like. But unfortunately, hockey's most severe critics these days are people who never go to a rink—or even watch a game on television—except when they're looking for a way of justifying their relentless criticism.

The game has far more one-trick ponies than it needs. They are people who target an aspect of the game they don't like and harp on it to the exclusion of everything else about the game, the good or the bad.

Rarely (if ever) mentioned is the fact that the average player's salary is in excess of $2 million U.S. and participation is totally voluntary. I will concede, as does Gino Odjick, the NHL's answer to Yogi Berra, that, "It's a hard way to make an easy living." But those who think the risk of injury is too great are free to find other jobs. Some of the critics hate the "hockey culture." Others don't like the fights. Some can't accept that a high-speed contact sport is certain to produce injuries. These people don't cover hockey. They cover their specific complaint. Again and again. Neither JD nor I have any respect for them.

"I can remember when I did the Rangers telecasts as the colour guy," JD said, "and for seven years in a row, they missed the playoffs with the highest payroll in the league. I'd get criticized for not ripping them. I wasn't being paid by the Rangers. I worked for the Madison Square Garden Network. But I said to myself, 'Why should I rip the Rangers all game long when the people who are watching are Rangers fans? Why would I want to have them turn against hockey? Why?' It didn't make any sense to me. That was my own personal philosophy and it was the same with *Hot Stove*. When I'd call players or general managers or Gary or Bill Daly or whoever it was, it wasn't to beat the heck out of things, it was to find stuff that was interesting and maybe use it."

As you might expect, JD, unlike me, rarely upset anyone in the hockey world. "Yeah, but I still used to have to field some calls because of you," he said laughing. "They'd say, 'You tell that guy he's full of shit for saying that.'"

The average person would have responded, "Tell him yourself. Do you want his phone number?" But JD is not your average person. He'd agree to tell me what they thought. The following Saturday, before the show got started, he would deliver his version of the message. "Hey, Big Boy, you really got that guy upset last week."

"Well, did he say that I was wrong?"

"No, but he says his wife didn't like it."

Then we'd laugh and get on with whatever we were doing.

For the most part, JD walked the straight and narrow. He had, and still has, friends at all levels of hockey and he saw no need to change that status. But he did make one misstep.

"The time I got into trouble was with Fox Sports," he recalled. "I loved working for Fox. They were fantastic. Big-time. But I was in Boston one Saturday and I went on the air with the *Hot Stove*. I had heard that when the Fox telecasts started, they were going to use a special puck that could tell viewers the speed it was travelling in miles per hour and all that stuff. I found that information fascinating, so I used it on the *Hot Stove*. It turned out that Fox hadn't announced it yet. I got my ass chewed out and rightly so. There is talk today about introducing certain innovations with the puck so they can track it and see whether it's over the goal line and all that. Fox was the first to think of innovations like that. I've still got a couple of those pucks that had sensors in them."

In the debate that ensued over the Fox pucks, JD took the stance that was appropriate for his designated role on *Hot Stove*. He acted like an American. Some people on Canadian TV [raises hand] were critical of the Fox approach to the game, especially the idea of leaving a coloured contrail to show where the puck had been. JD wasn't opposed to it. He still isn't.

"The only thing I wish was different," he said, "was that I would have liked to see something on the remote control that allowed viewers to watch the game with the glowing puck or watch it without the glowing puck. Being a Canadian, what I didn't understand was that most of the negative reaction to the puck itself was from Canada. For what reason? They didn't even watch it. They were watching Canadian TV."

But it was never really about viewing preferences. It had to do with the concept of Americans changing what we perceive as our game. It was the fear that glowing pucks were the thin edge of the wedge. Fox had also expressed a desire to have the game played in four quarters, or perhaps two halves, rather than three periods.

Sure, these initial changes were being made with American viewers in mind, but how long would it be before the U.S. TV moguls became the arbiters of what was right and wrong with hockey and imposed their "innovations" on Canada?

"It wasn't screwing the game up," insisted JD. "It didn't make the game any different. Fox just wanted to teach people who didn't understand the game, and show them where the puck was. They were thinking along those lines. They were trying to expand the fan base."

There was also the matter of Transformer-like creatures that zoomed onto the screen when goals were scored.

"The testing they did with younger people showed that they loved the robots," said JD. "They loved the flaming puck with the trail and all that stuff. But it went away. It was a major marvel to me that they were able to do that at the time. It was fascinating."

Perhaps it was fascinating. So is the bull running in Pamplona. That doesn't mean I want a herd of cattle released onto the ice after every goal.

But JD refused to back down. "You also have to change the game to make it grow," he maintained. "The simple aspect of it all was that

Fox was trying to grow the game in the United States. It had nothing to do with Canada."

We still differ on that point, but there were also points on which we strongly agreed. There was, for instance, the time that Rick Westhead, another occasional pundit on *Hot Stove*, who has never done anything to disprove the theory that he hates hockey, was given all the time he needed to breathlessly inform the viewers that a new Russian hockey league was being formed. Westhead, one of Ron MacLean's favourites, insisted that within five years the Kontinental Hockey League would surpass the NHL in popularity, talent, profit, and every other worthwhile aspect. That was in 2007.

"That is actually humorous," chuckled JD when the subject arose. "That is so outrageous that you just laugh. There's one league that's the best league in the world. That's the National Hockey League and that's not going to change. This is where the whole world of hockey players wants to come and play."

JD and I also agreed that NHL rinks need to be wider.

"Yeah, I got a kick out of Brian Burke about two years ago saying we should make the rinks wider," JD said. "Not the size they use in the Olympics, but like Finland, where they're a hybrid. They're about eight feet wider. I told Brian, 'Well, we said that on *Hot Stove* fifteen or twenty years ago.'"

You never knew what you were going to get on that show. Sometimes it was light, but usually (Westhead aside), we were far ahead of the crowd when it came to news and opinions. "I don't know why," said JD, "but it worked. People enjoyed it. Imagine if they had Twitter back then. Twitter would be flooded with our stuff. You know what it did? It created interesting talk. That was good. We gave our opinions, and those opinions created discussions around the water coolers in offices everywhere. They were good.

"And Grapes [Don Cherry] was gigantic then, too, on *Coach's Corner*. People really enjoyed those two intermissions."

JD is one of the few TV personalities who can look at the medium from the inside, but also see it from the point of view of both a player and a president. As of this writing, he is the president of the New York Rangers.

He's like one of those people—and most of us know at least one—who grew up in one country then moved to another. As the years go by, they travel back and forth, and even though they're not unhappy in either country, they're always missing aspects of the other.

JD knew where I was going with this. "I miss television," he said. "I do. But I really like what I'm doing. When you retire as a player at twenty-eight or twenty-nine like I did, you wonder what you're going to do. You think, 'Oh. Okay, there's television. Let's see what I can do now that I'm on my own.' But you learn that it's a team game. You watch the intermission show like we used to have and there are dozens and dozens of people who put that thing together to make it work so you can watch it. It's very similar to a hockey team. You've got a general manager who's the producer, you've got a coach who's the director, so you learn, okay, you're part of their team.

"*Hot Stove* was part of the fabric at the time for people to watch. A lot of times, I'd go out for a beer or just go to get gas in my car and people were watching. They were fans. That made me feel good. It was a lot like being a player and at the same time, I enjoyed all the guys I worked with. Every one of them. Doing five Winter Olympics was great. Fascinating. I miss it, but I have no complaints whatsoever. I think of all the people I met along the way. Great people. Awesome."

But despite how much JD enjoyed his time with *Hot Stove*, like the rest of us, he experienced a little tension in the moments immediately preceding the show.

"It's the game of the week," JD said, "and being a part of it, I always had butterflies because it was live or live-to-tape. You didn't want to mess up. You wanted to have fun. You wanted to bring new ideas. And afterwards, John Shannon would call us and say, 'This was great.' Or, 'That one could have been improved,' or whatever. He was always trying to help us, trying to make it better. It was special because it was *Hockey Night in Canada*. And it was hockey night in Canada."

CHAPTER 13

Trouble in Paradise

The years that *Hot Stove* was under the direction of John Shannon were the glory days. The show had a focus. It gave hockey fans the information they wanted, and it was entertaining. There were scoops, arguments, jokes, speculation, and sometimes good old-fashioned gossip.

Shannon always said, "You don't want everybody to be the same," so we all had our roles. Eric Duhatschek, who gradually took over from Jim Hughson as the western representative, put it this way: "I was more circumspect than you were, Strach. When the lineup was you, me, JD, and MacLean, I always thought that MacLean was the traffic cop. He might contribute to the conversation. He might not. JD was a former player, so he could bring that insight. You were the guy wearing the black hat. You were the bad guy. You were the gunslinger. You were the person that they loved to hate. And I thought of myself as the information guy, so I basically just stepped in and passed along information."

That was a fairly accurate evaluation. I was smug, direct, sometimes insulting. I still remember the look of shock and horror on JD's face when I called New York Islanders forward Mariusz Czerkawski a floater. He did a genuine double take. As a former player, JD would never stoop that low. He would never be that straightforward in discussing a player's attributes, or the lack of them.

But what a lot of people don't understand about television is that it's not about rapport, it's about numbers. People would write letters to Shannon saying something like, "I can't stand that Strachan asshole. He's so arrogant. I shout at the television every week when he's on." John would be delighted.

Don Cherry provided a perfect example. There were more commercials built around his segment than any other eight minutes in television. Why? Because people were watching. Sure, many of them were watching so they could deride Don the next time his name came up in a conversation, or criticize him on their next social media post. But they were watching. And to an advertiser, that's all that matters.

I mentioned earlier that in 1980, when I was offered a columnist's job at the *Globe and Mail*, I originally turned it down because the other columnist, Allen Abel, was, and still is, such a beautiful writer. I felt that it would be something like going up on a stage with a kazoo to accompany Mark Knopfler. "We don't want you to be another Allen," the *Globe* people said. "We've already got him."

Instead, they told me what they wanted, and they built an advertising campaign around me. It touted "Strachan on sports." There was a head shot as part of it. Behind a pair of glasses and a faint, droopy moustache, and under well-groomed hair—all of which are long gone now—was my face. "Opinionated. Infuriating. Entertaining," read the copy alongside. I didn't anticipate much difficulty living up to the first two, and I assumed the third would follow pretty well automatically.

We had pigeonholes for our mail in the *Globe* office and the routine didn't vary much. Allen would wander over and forlornly pick out a solitary letter—or turn away on seeing an empty box—and, head down, go back to his desk. I'd go over and try to pry out the bundle of letters that were wedged into my pigeonhole.

Was it because I was a better writer than Allen? Give your head a shake. It was because I stirred people's emotions. I never lied about anything and the letters rarely complained about factual errors. But I evaluated situations and gave my opinion, whether it would be widely accepted or not. And unlike some columnists, I gave my honest opinion, and not something I threw out just to attract attention (and which might be the opposite of what I said so fervently a week before). This approach required what Mike Milbury refers to as "a thick crust," but as far as I'm concerned, there's no shame in it.

John Shannon understood television. His immediate successors did not. John knew that, ironically, the popularity of a panel show is not based on the popularity of all of its panelists. John Davidson holds a similar opinion.

"In my opinion, John Shannon is a television genius," he said. "He's creative, innovative, and above all that, his ego, as far as I know, whether he was working with me or with others, didn't get in the way. He was always a team player. Sometimes he'd have information and he'd pass it along. There aren't very many people like that. He was anything but a selfish person and that made for a better show.

"I remember when he was the western producer doing Calgary Flames games and we would record the openings. Sometimes I'd do twenty-five takes because I screwed it up. You wanted to kill him by the end of it, but we were going to keep doing it until we got it right."

Had we been at another network, *Hot Stove*, under Shannon's stewardship, would probably have sailed along unsullied for a few more years. Perhaps a decade. Maybe it would still be running. But we weren't at another network. We were at the Canadian Broadcasting Corporation, which never, in its entire television history, has been able to come to terms with the fact that its mandate is to serve the viewers, not to politicize them.

If you think I'm arrogant, you should meet the people in the upper echelons of the CBC. For the most part, they hate sports and look down their noses at the fans. They almost lost *Hockey Night in Canada* to CTV in 1988 as a result of that attitude. On that occasion, they caved in to the demands of Molstar, the subsidiary of Molson Breweries Ltd. They "reevaluated" their principles in order to keep *Hockey Night*. And it wasn't because they were concerned about losing the revenue that the show generated. More likely, they were concerned about bragging rights: we are the CBC and of course we have the top-rated show in the country.

And maybe there wasn't anything really wrong with that. They would have been saving the taxpayers some money for once. But the pervasive sports-loathing attitude wasn't defeated. It just retreated for a little while and lurked in the background waiting for an opportunity to reemerge.

In 2000, there were some ominous shuffles in the high levels of the CBC. The first was the departure of Alan Clark. I've frequently mentioned all the changes that John Shannon made to *Hockey Night*. But it stands to reason that someone above him had to approve those changes. John was well up in CBC sports, but he wasn't the head. Alan Clark was.

Personally, I didn't have a lot to do with Alan. I'd see him once in a while on some of the road trips and exchange pleasantries, but we were nothing more than acquaintances. That was Alan's style. He stayed at his own corporate level, which was far above mine.

"Alan was a great boss," Shannon recalled. "He said to me, 'You know more about hockey than I do. You know all about this TV side. You go ahead and do it.'" Clark was more at home in the CBC boardrooms than in the studio.

"He understood the CBC much better than I did," Shannon conceded, "and he wanted to change the show so that it was a CBC show rather than a Molstar show."

I hate to jump around too much, but I think it's necessary here to establish the relationship between John and Alan, and tell a story about when John first got the job.

Like his sidekick Kathy Broderick, John finished high school and took the radio-television arts program at Ryerson Polytechnic Institute. As part of the course, he decided to write a feature article for the Ryerson magazine on Jim Robson, the legendary Vancouver Canucks announcer. He needed *Hockey Night*'s permission for the project, and was told that it would only be forthcoming if he offered them the opportunity to see the finished product before it was published.

Hockey Night management saw that article in May 1978, and in October they called John and offered him a job as a runner. He got ten dollars a game—that's ten more than Kathy got per night a couple of years later, if you remember.

Under the tutelage of Ralph Mellanby, John worked his way up to being the western producer of *Hockey Night in Canada* until that fateful game in 1986 when he decided to let viewers see the end of the game they'd been watching for three hours, and therefore delayed the CBC news by two minutes. That got him fired.

He had no trouble getting other jobs. He worked for Global TV, did the Minnesota North Stars telecasts for a while, and in 1994, produced the Lillehammer Olympics for CTV. It was around that time that the CBC decided that it wanted its own executive producer on *Hockey Night in Canada*, instead of leaving it to Molstar.

John applied, but he didn't think he had much chance. He knew that he was not highly regarded, to put it mildly, by Alan Clark, who was one of the three people doing the interviews.

"Alan was adamant that there was no way I was going to get the job," Shannon recalled. "He didn't even want to talk to me. He had heard I was a hothead. But Doug Sellers, who was a good friend of mine, said to him, 'You'd better interview this guy.' So I went to a CBC interview where the head of CBC human resources, Alan, and a lady named Phyllis Platt were in the room.

"I sat at the head of the table without as much as a piece of paper for three hours and went through the whole show with them. I went through every person on the show. I told them where the show needed to go. I told them what needed to happen. I told them how passionate I was to change it, and how passionate I was to make *Hockey Night* what it used to be.

"I guess I impressed them. I still have Phyllis's handwritten letter saying this was the greatest interview she'd ever been part of. The next day I got a phone call from Alan. He said, 'We have to meet.' We met at a little restaurant at Yonge and St. Clair. He offered me the job." John chuckled as he recalled the incident. "This is after two months of him saying he didn't even want to interview me for the job, let alone give it to me.

"I had a really good relationship with the guy. There was a lot we could do. TSN didn't have anything like they have today with all their channels, and Sportsnet wasn't even on the air then. So we went to doubleheaders, and we were starting to create programming between periods and between games. We had so much programming, we needed to do a pregame show. So we added a half-hour pregame show."

I asked Shannon how Clark had reacted to the idea of doing doubleheaders.

"As a matter of fact, he had thought of it himself, too," said John. "It was just a matter of us agreeing at the same time that it was the right thing to do." That decision led to a little more preparatory work of a technological nature, but Shannon had an answer for that as well.

"The national news was on the air at six, so I went to them and said, 'Could you spare a news crew for an hour at three?' They did and it only cost us one thousand dollars. I don't think the crew was too happy. They had a pretty simple life at the CBC in those days."

In the meantime, Clark was concerning himself with the corporate side. He was now able to go into the boardroom and point out that a full 50 percent of the network's weekly revenue came from the seven hours of *Hockey Night in Canada*. (As an aside, the next-largest money producer was *Coronation Street*, the British soap opera.)

Those were the good years, and the relationship between John and Alan was key to the show's innovations and success. Which takes us back to the year 2000 and the arrival on the scene of two people who started *Hot Stove* on its downward slide—Nancy Lee and Harold Redekopp.

Nancy Lee had started at the CBC in 1987 as a sports reporter and had the acumen to immediately recognize that in a fervently politically correct workplace like the CBC, leaning towards feminist issues would do her no harm. As a result, it took her only until 1994 to become head of CBC Radio sports, which, at the time, was highly acclaimed. You'd never know it by listening to CBC Radio now, but it had a wide range of sports shows and even used to have NHL game broadcasts on Sunday night.

In two years, Lee dismantled it to the point that it was a shell of its former self, and was down to what was basically a half hour of female-oriented programming on Saturday afternoon. In fact, CBC Radio sports had shrunk so much that it no longer needed anyone to run it.

The CBC had to put her somewhere, so in 1996, they made her the deputy head of CBC sports. To those who didn't know her full background, she appeared to be a star on the rise—from rookie to deputy department head in only nine years. Like many others, Harold Redekopp, who was a vice president of English-language television at CBC, took notice. After four years, he made her the executive director of CBC Sports. That meant she was in charge of *Hockey Night*. It needs to be said that he had long expressed a loathing for *Hockey Night in Canada* during his CBC career.

"Harold Redekopp brought Nancy in to replace Alan because he didn't like the direction the sports department was going in," explained Shannon.

Redekopp had been in his VP post for two years after running CBC Radio, which during his tenure had an unexplained $3.5 million shortfall one year. An investigation was promised, but ultimately there were no recriminations. It was only the taxpayers' money, after all. Regardless, he had been one of Lee's superiors at CBC Radio and he knew he could count on her to join him in his campaign to minimize the impact of sports on CBC television.

Once in the new position, Lee made it clear what her priorities would be. "Now that we've established ourselves as executives, the big challenge now is getting women on TV where they will be seen," she said when interviewed by the *Toronto Star*. "The sad thing is that [women in sports] is still a story. It's my job to make sure that in ten, fifteen, twenty years' time, that it's still not as much of a story." No mention was made of improving the sports coverage offered to the network's viewers.

"In the summer of 2000 my contract expired," recalled Shannon. Around the TV world, John Shannon was known as the best hockey producer on the planet. But Nancy Lee refused to renew his contract.

"I think she thought we were an island unto ourselves, and we weren't part of the CBC sports department," Shannon said. "To my mind, Alan did a great job with CBC sports department but now it was about to be changed."

In the next few years, Lee subjected CBC television sports to the same treatment she had inflicted on CBC Radio sports. You might call it a dismantling. Actually, it was more of a dismembering. She fired Chris Cuthbert—to this day one of the elite announcers on Canadian television—citing budgetary concerns. Although, she wasn't too worried about budgetary concerns when she and her assistant ran up a bill of $8,590 for five days at the Kempinski Hotel in Berlin, in 2006. Furthermore, Chris had agreed to take a period of temporary unpaid leave to save his job. It was to no avail.

She fired Brian Williams, another mainstay who had been at the CBC for more than thirty years. She fired Paul Graham, one of the top-flight producers on *Hockey Night*. He ended up being in charge of the Toronto Raptors telecasts on another network.

She even fired Ron MacLean. Oops. Bad move, Nancy. There was an uproar from coast to coast as CBC viewers expressed their outrage. Her decision became front-page news in every daily paper in the country. Protests were staged and the demand for CBC accountability was such that the matter had to be kicked upstairs for review—not a normal occurrence, to say the least.

The CBC tended to give its edicts the gravity and authority of papal bulls. As such, they were accorded the status of total infallibility. But on this occasion, Lee was overruled and the announcement of Ron's firing was withdrawn.

Strangely enough, I wasn't invited to sit in on the meeting at which Lee had to explain herself. I imagine it went something like this:

"I never watch that hockey show of yours, Nancy, but isn't this MacWhatsit fellow tremendously popular?"

"It's Ron MacLean. Yes, he is."

"And that, what do you call it, *Hockey Night in Canada*? Isn't it by far our most watched and most profitable show?"

"Yes, it is."

"Then why on earth would you fire him?"

"Did you read the interview the *Toronto Star* did with me?"

"In the sports pages?"

"Yes."

"Nancy! Really!"

"Sorry. Well, I kind of explained it there. I thought it would be good to have a woman hosting a hockey show. All the players are male. All the executives are male. Most of the viewers are male. I thought it was a good time to make them aware of the error of their ways."

"Get him back."

Nancy Lee was not a quick learner. Later, apparently having been totally infected with that curious CBC malaise that imbues executives with a sense of invulnerability and invincibility—then adds an inherent sense of unerring judgment—she told Don Cherry she was going to fire him when his contract expired in 2004. At least she knew she would have Redekopp's backing for that one. In 2003, Cherry had expressed support for the American invasion of Iraq and Redekopp was furious.

"We have made it clear to both Don and Ron that *Coach's Corner* is not an appropriate place to air opinions about the Iraq War," he said in a CBC bull.

But Cherry did repeat his opinions on an American radio show. Redekopp said he couldn't fire Cherry for that transgression because he hadn't made his statements on the CBC, but he certainly wasn't pleased. "We think it showed bad judgment and we frankly wish he hadn't said it," he said.

Redekopp was also the CBC executive who instituted a seven-second delay on the broadcasts of *Coach's Corner* so that he could prevent the dissemination of remarks he thought were controversial. The specific incident that prompted that action was Don's 2004 announcement that he didn't like players wearing visors. "Most of the guys that wear them are Europeans or French guys," he said.

Redekopp blasted Cherry for "reprehensible and personal" comments. In a press release, he said that CBC "categorically rejects and denounces his opinions." The press release went on to say, "Fans across the country have tuned into *Hockey Night in Canada*'s *Coach's Corner* for over twenty years because of his insights and understanding of the game."

So what were we to deduce from that? For twenty years, fans had been idiots for tuning in to hear Don's opinions, which the CBC categorically rejects and denounces? Who knows? But what we do know is that after Shannon left *Hockey Night*, and was no longer able to insulate Don from upper-level interference, Cherry was repeatedly summoned to Redekopp's office. Their meetings were never pleasant.

"I thought hockey was a vicious occupation," laughed Cherry when the subject was broached. "This was ten times worse than hockey."

No doubt Redekopp was less than impressed when Don later pointed out that the arithmetic was undeniable. Most of the guys wearing visors were indeed either European or French Canadian. Don had been wrong, it seems, for stating a "reprehensible and personal" fact. Nowadays, every player has developed a booming shot, the effect of which is further enhanced by the use of composite sticks, and as a result, visors have become the norm. But in 2004, the necessity for them was nowhere near as pronounced.

Although Don always made light of it over the years, his battles with Redekopp bothered him. He didn't want to lose his job, but if it had to happen, a resignation or contract termination might be marginally acceptable. But the possibility of losing the battle to a dismissal at the hands of Harold Redekopp horrified him. Nevertheless, he didn't let it show.

"I know Nancy Lee didn't like me," he said in fall 2019. "And she was in his hip pocket so I had no support there. I remember when Redekopp was getting near to retirement, and he said to me, 'I'll be gone in a month and the legend that I want to leave is that I was the guy who got rid of you. I'm going to do it.' I said, 'Yeah? We'll see.'"

There was always a bond between *Hot Stove* and *Coach's Corner*. Shannon hadn't created the latter, but his mentor, Ralph Mellanby, had. And if there was ever anything Mellanby did that Shannon disliked, I never heard about it. Ron MacLean was the host of both shows.

We all had the same set and the same production crews. All the *Hot Stove* regulars liked Don.

Don always watched our show, sometimes from his greenroom, sometimes from the sidelines just out of camera range, and afterwards he would offer his comments. He sometimes wasn't happy about our stories. I think the one that irked him the most was the one in which I reported that Mike Gillis was in line to become the general manager of the Vancouver Canucks. Don crossed paths with Gillis over the years and didn't like him in the least. But his unhappiness never extended to the people on *Hot Stove*, just the developments we sometimes revealed. He was one of our biggest fans and enjoyed the way we interacted.

Eventually, those who champion liberal causes, but only accept free speech when it agrees with their own principles, got rid of Don. He had been in their sights for years and in November 2019, they finally did what Harold Redekopp and Nancy Lee couldn't do. They got Don fired.

It was November 9, and as was the case with every *Coach's Corner* immediately preceding Remembrance Day, Don made a plea for viewers to purchase the poppies that fund the Canadian Legion, and hence military veterans. He was not wearing one of his trademark outrageous jackets on this occasion, just a black blazer emblazoned with the Royal Canadian Legion crest—and, of course, a poppy. A few years earlier, he had lambasted the general population, saying that "you people" should buy poppies. In 2019, he again referred to "you people," a phrase he uses often.

This time, he preceded it with the observation that poppy sales were lower in Toronto than in the smaller cities. "Forget it with downtown Toronto. Nobody wears the poppy. . . . You people that come here, whatever it is, you love our way of life, you love our milk and honey, at least you can pay a couple of bucks for a poppy or something like that. These guys paid for your way of life that you enjoy in Canada. These guys paid the biggest price."

Was he being critical of immigrants? The case could be made. The most recent census prior to that version of *Coach's Corner* showed

that 46.1 percent of Torontonians were born in a country other than Canada. And having lived in Toronto for a significant portion of my life, and having travelled around the country extensively, I can attest that poppy-wearing in Canada's largest city is nowhere near as widespread as it is in smaller cities. So if Don says "you people that come here" about those on the streets in Toronto, he's talking about almost half of the population.

But was it racist? Don didn't single out nonwhite immigrants. Toronto has a high proportion of Eastern Europeans as well as many others who would make up that 46.1 percent. Many are Americans. So really, what he did was criticize immigrants who hadn't bought a poppy. In earlier shows, he had criticized *everyone* who hadn't bought a poppy. Unless you believe immigrants should be exempt from criticism, he hadn't done anything he hadn't done before.

But the media jumped on it as a "racist rant." It may have been a rant. Most *Coach's Corner* segments were. But racist? Only if you want it to be. And many of the media observers did. As is the case with most people who find themselves subjected to trial by media, Cherry was quickly convicted and sentenced.

On Monday, Bart Yabsley, the president of Sportsnet, said: "Sports brings people together—it unites us, not divides us. Following further discussions with Don Cherry after Saturday night's broadcast, it has been decided it is the right time for him to immediately step down. During the broadcast, he made divisive remarks that do not represent our values or what we stand for."

Don had opened his controversial 2019 segment by saying that he was not sure that he would once again run the Remembrance Day vignette that he made years earlier after visiting World War I battlefields in France, even though it had evolved into something of a *Coach's Corner* tradition. However, a veteran had urged him to run it for those who buy poppies. After his comments about Toronto, Don announced that he was "[g]onna run it again for you great people [that phrase again] and great Canadians that bought a poppy."

Ron Maclean gave Don a thumbs-up and said, "I love you for it." Twenty-four hours later, Ron had lost his love. By then, he was hosting the *Hometown Hockey* telecast and throwing Don under the bus in order to save his own skin. "Don Cherry made remarks which were hurtful, discriminatory, which were flat-out wrong," he said. He apologized and apologized some more on behalf of the network.

The next Saturday, on *Hockey Night in Canada*, MacLean said, "There were steps that needed to be taken because of what had been said by Don, and he didn't want to do those steps so he made his choice and I made mine." The steps in question were an apology from Don, which he refused to provide. He felt he had done nothing wrong.

"I said 'everybody' and I meant everybody," Don explained in a TV interview a couple of days later. "Everybody that comes to this country should honour our fallen dead and somehow, it has been misinterpreted and this is what happens." To Don, his situation was similar to one that often arises on TV crime shows. A suspect is offered a reduced sentence if he pleads guilty, but refuses because he believes himself to be innocent.

On *Hometown Hockey*, MacLean went on to say, "And then the next choice, which was a *really* hard choice—probably the sleepless nights all week are mostly about this—Don's my guy. I'm in a foxhole with Don and I've decided to go one way and he another." Fortunately for all of us, the soldiers for whom Don exhibited his concern had a different definition of what it means to be a foxhole guy.

It seems pretty clear that, as far as the general populace was concerned, the situation became this: If you agreed with what Don said, you could point out that his view was founded in fact. If you didn't agree with what Don said, you could interpret it to make it offensive. And across the country, that's what happened.

Although it was never reported—and it certainly wasn't Don who told me this—Yabsley went to Cherry's house in the hope that a face-to-face plea would bring about a compromise. He had caved to public pressure but he knew Don's value on the show and didn't want to lose him. He asked Don to apologize. He wouldn't.

Yabsley's next proposal was that Don would agree to take a sensitivity course. This development would then be announced on *Hockey Night in Canada* and the new Don Cherry would return to *Coach's Corner*. That proposal was not well received. Somewhere, Nancy Lee was probably giving a fist pump. Even though she didn't finish the job, she transformed CBC Sports in much the same way that a tornado transforms a trailer park.

For generations, going back to the day when *Hockey Night in Canada* moved from radio to television, CBC had been the go-to network for Canadian sports fans. If a big sporting event was coming up, you rarely needed to check the listings. It would be on the CBC.

During Nancy Lee's tenure, the CBC lost the right to valuable properties in almost every popular sport. She lost football (the Grey Cup), curling (the Brier and the Tournament of Hearts), baseball (Toronto Blue Jays), motor racing (the Toronto Indy and the Vancouver Indy), and hockey (a large portion of the NHL playoffs).

Furthermore, the CBC had always been the network of record for the Olympics, but Nancy Lee lost those rights as well: not only the 2012 summer games in London, England, but even the 2010 Winter Olympics in Vancouver. All this came about even though Nancy Lee had created a new position within CBC Sports—director of program acquisitions!

Lee left the CBC in 2006 to work as chief operating officer of the host broadcast team for the 2010 Winter Olympics in Vancouver. By then, though, it was too late to repair the damage that had been done to *Hockey Night in Canada*, and by extension, to *Satellite Hot Stove*.

One night, I was knocking back a pint or two with a TSN star who wouldn't want to be identified. We talked about our respective jobs and the subject of Nancy Lee arose. "She was the best thing that ever happened to our network," he said.

CHAPTER 14

Filling the Gap

After John Shannon left in 2000, *Hot Stove* started to move in a different direction, and as a result, it featured a constantly changing parade of panelists. Some of them lasted only one or two shows, while others made a few appearances, but didn't last.

Far too many were totally unsuited for the type of show *Hot Stove* was meant to be. Some of them qualified as insiders—Sean Burke and Scott Mellanby, for instance. They had graduated from NHL rosters and worked their way up to the management level.

But the show's aim was to tell viewers what was going on in the hockey world. These guys certainly had the requisite knowledge, but there was no chance they would share it with the public. Their jobs required them to be closemouthed.

Murray Wilson and Brian Hayward also made appearances. Again, they were former NHL players, so they knew the game. But once more, even though the knowledge was there, it wasn't going to be revealed to the audience. Both of them were team announcers and therefore team employees. And when you have a job like that, you're expected to present nothing but sugar-sweet views of the NHL.

Don't get me wrong. I liked all these people and count them as friends. Furthermore, they were good at their primary jobs. But they weren't going to fulfill the vision that John Shannon had established for *Hot Stove*.

Aside from various team staff, a few newspaper beat writers made cameo appearances. Usually this was in response to a development that had received a lot of attention during the week but concerned only one franchise. A writer from the city in question would be called in for the day, but he wouldn't be expected to contribute anything that did not directly relate to that high-profile story.

Regardless of who they were or where they came from, one thing remained true. As is the case with any job, you could get away with a mistake if you had seniority, but not if you were still in the tryout stage.

John McKeachie, as warm-hearted a guy as you're ever likely to meet, proved this to be true in a rather unfortunate fashion. It was decided that he would fill the role as the western representative one day, and his primary contribution had to do with a highly regarded potential free agent that the Vancouver Canucks coveted. McKeachie, who hosted a radio show in Vancouver, assured us that the kid was determined to come out of college and join the NHL, and that soon, perhaps even that very day, he would sign with the Canucks. We taped the show at 3 p.m. that day and by the time it aired, around 8:30, the kid was indeed in the NHL. He was the property of the New York Islanders.

The announcement had been made about 6 p.m. but with JD off fulfilling his duties with the Rangers, there was no way we could rerecord. We had to go with McKeachie's mistake and an explanation about the show being taped in the afternoon. No one considers that to be good television. That was McKeachie's last appearance on *Hot Stove*.

Speaking of changes, in 2005 I was given my first extended vacation from *Hockey Night in Canada*. Nobody mentioned anything I'd done wrong. There was no written notification, just a phone call from Joel Darling, the executive producer at the time, saying they "had decided to move in a different direction."

To replace me, Pierre LeBrun was brought in and given the status of regular panelist. It would have been hard for them to make a better choice. Pierre covered hockey for the Canadian Press, the country's primary wire service. For the most part, that meant he had been hired to fill in the blanks on the mandatory story format that, for as long as anyone cared to remember, had been something like this:

Two goals from (player's name here) led the (winning team's name) to a (insert score) victory over the (losing team's name) in a (adjective to describe pace) game at the (arena name) last night.

Once the basics had been provided in the opening paragraph, the writer was expected to sprinkle in a few specifics, as well as some supporting quotes from coaches and players. End of job.

But Pierre changed that approach—one that had been in place for most of a century. He treated his job as if he were a hockey columnist for a newspaper. He broke stories. He fleshed out others. He speculated on likely implications and developments.

Little wonder, then, that we became friends. Even though I worked for a paper and he was with a wire service, we could share information to our mutual benefit. The year before he came to *Hot Stove*, in 2004, the NHL staged hockey's first World Cup. For that we were in each other's company almost every day. Including training camp, the tournament ran about five weeks and with the NHL lockout looming, it made sense to put in workdays before the league shut down. So we took no days off.

But our relationship went far beyond the job. We lived only a few blocks apart in the area of Toronto known as the Annex and therefore frequented the same watering holes. On Sunday afternoons, we often travelled to a more central pub where we would meet a host of friends and watch the NFL games. This pub had a few televisions and the owner turned over the remote controls to our group. It is one of Pierre's great failings that he remains a fan of the Dallas Cowboys, no matter how many times I point out their deficiencies to him or explain why the Pittsburgh Steelers are vastly superior.

In the course of writing this book, I asked him to talk about his time on *Hot Stove*. If it seems a bit formal, it's because Pierre was aware that it was being recorded and his views were to be part of a book. I assure you that he speaks quite differently most of the time, and if it involves his other primary concerns—his sports pools, the Cowboys, or the need for another round—the volume level is ratcheted up as well.

Pierre had just covered the 2004–05 NHL lockout for the Canadian Press, which he saw as a major moment for his career, when, like me, he got a call from Joel Darling. The call came as a surprise.

"I was thirty-two years old, had done a bit of TV at *The Score* since 2003, but really, my experience was as a writer since 1995 at the Canadian Press. The lockout no doubt raised my profile, I guess. But never did I think that the executive producer of *Hockey Night* would be calling me at that point. There were certainly no rumours suggesting that.

"It was about a week before the season, too. Joel offered me the chance to be part of *Hot Stove*. What a rush! I immediately thought of my late mother, who had passed away in 1998 of ALS at fifty-four years old. She was a huge hockey fan and she would have been so proud. I'm not going to lie, I was fighting back tears.

"But I had mixed feelings when I realized the *Hot Stove* opportunity was at the expense of Al Strachan, a friend and mentor. My first call after talking to Darling was to my dad, who was thrilled.

"My second call was to Strach to make sure he was okay with it. Had Strach raised any objections, believe it or not, I would have passed. But Al told me if anyone should replace him, it should be me."

Naturally, I was upset at being eased out for no reason, but if the job was no longer mine, I felt that Pierre might as well have it. My reasoning was that they weren't going to leave the chair empty and I'd rather see Pierre in that seat, not one of the charlatans who pretend to be knowledgeable but aren't. My memory of the call is that Pierre opened by saying, "You're going to hate me for this." Once he told me about Darling's call, I quickly assured him that he had my blessing.

Pierre was smart enough to limit his early *Hot Stove* contributions to basic facts he had dug up, without tossing in his views.

"As the rookie on *Hot Stove*, I definitely didn't see my role as the guy who should stir the drink," he explained. "I just wanted to keep my head down and bring the information to the table. As I've gotten older, I've obviously grown more comfortable taking a stance and having an opinion. My nine years at ESPN.com helped develop that. But at the time, as a young guy on *Hot Stove*, my approach was, bring the info—and that's it. I was in awe of working alongside Ron MacLean. I always thought he was just an absolute magician in his job as *HNIC* host."

Pierre spent six years as a regular on *Hot Stove*. Once Joel Darling left, he was replaced by Sherali Najak and I was quickly recalled to the show (more on that later). Once we were working together, Pierre and I contacted our respective sources on many a Saturday afternoon to make sure the content was what we felt it ought to be.

During that period, *Hot Stove* probably had more pure information packed into its eight minutes than it had ever had. If the full package on a Saturday night was Pierre, Scott Morrison, Eric Duhatschek, and me, very few NHL developments of consequence remained unexposed—if any. We were all veterans; we were all hockey junkies; we all knew every person of consequence in the NHL and we were all proud to be part of *Hot Stove*.

As it happened, Pierre was one of the few to express concern when I was writing my book *Why the Leafs Suck and How They Can Be Fixed.* He warned that it might lead to a significant negative reaction. I didn't disagree. After all, a large percentage of the things I wrote resulted in a negative reaction. But being used to it, I shrugged off his warning. Because he had so many solid sources in the hockey world, I always thought that somebody might have tipped him off that I was going to get into hot water, but he says not.

"I don't remember anyone actually saying anything to me," he said. "It was more just a gut feeling on my part that the book would bring you trouble at *HNIC*. I was worried for you. You were always the best at stirring the pot. I just had a feeling that the book might push it too far."

Pierre left *Hot Stove* in 2011—and voluntarily, which is not the usual way people departed.

"My wife and I had a two-year-old with twins on the way," he explained. "I needed to reclaim Saturdays for my family. Mark Milliere called me from TSN during the 2011 playoffs and offered me a chance to work as one of their insiders along with Bob McKenzie and Darren Dreger. I was going to have a Monday-to-Friday existence during the regular season. It was a no-brainer.

"Bob was someone I had always looked up to and modelled my career after. When it came to being a writer who transitioned to full-time TV, he was the best; and Dregs was a peer I had so much respect for. Why not join forces?

"It has been a great relationship ever since. And the timing was perfect from a family perspective. But I do remember someone at *HNIC* telling me when I told them of my decision, 'No one ever leaves *Hockey Night*.' He was probably right. But it made sense for me."

It was definitely the right approach to take. Because of TSN's ties with ESPN in the United States, a new world was opened to Pierre and he made the most of it. With his first language being French, he has also been able to carve out a niche on RDS, the French-language branch of TSN.

When he started on *Hot Stove*, the show had lost some of its lustre. Darling was a good producer, but he did not have the kind of hockey mentality required to supervise a hockey-oriented production. The segment was foundering, but Pierre's involvement supplied it with a cornerstone. Week after week, he brought solid knowledge to the fore, knowledge that simply was not forthcoming from some of the other panelists.

TSN, being in an expansion phase, noticed all this and gave him a chance to become a part of their operation. Stepping in as my replacement turned out to be a major development in his career. I didn't know the specifics at the time, but I knew that it was the right move and I certainly wasn't about to discourage it.

CHAPTER 15

Over-Under

In journalism, whether it's the televised kind or the printed kind, the need to protect sources is paramount. If you want to get good information, you have to assure the source that he will not be identified. If you don't do that, the fear of revenge or recrimination will almost certainly convince a potential source that he should keep his information to himself.

But when a controversial story breaks, there is always a reaction from those who are at the centre of it. They would love to retaliate by attacking the source, but since he's not available, they go after the messenger. That would be me. There were a number of *Hot Stove* incidents that got me in trouble, but one of the leaders in that regard was the Barry Melrose affair in 2008.

Even though it was still early in the season, October 25 to be precise, I said that the Tampa Bay Lightning's on-ice problems were significant, and improvement was not likely because those problems were inevitable in such a totally dysfunctional organization. But there was more. I expanded on that point, saying I had it on very good authority that Len Barrie, one of the team's owners, had gone into the dressing room and given some young players instructions on how he wanted them to respond to certain situations that might arise during a game, especially with regard to penalty killing and power play. In short, he had taken over the coach's duty.

Naturally enough, Mike Milbury got upset when I made these allegations. There was nothing unusual about this. Milbury got upset at a lot of things I said. As a former player, Milbury was sensitive to player-related issues that he felt should not be revealed to the media. As a former coach, he was sensitive to issues that involved meddling on the part of an owner. Therefore, he was doubly sensitive about this Tampa Bay item.

He suggested, as he was known to do, that I was wrong. No new ground had been broken there. But what elevated the matter to another level was the subsequent reaction of the Lightning coach, Barry Melrose, who got a lot more upset about it than Milbury. He, too, flatly denied the story and was much stronger in his condemnation than Milbury had been. When asked by a *Tampa Tribune* reporter about the allegation of owner interference, Melrose said, "Al is sort of like a spaghetti salesman. He just throws so much against the wall and hopes something sticks, and it usually doesn't stick. It's BS and Al thrives on BS. It's total lies."

(Do spaghetti salesmen really throw their product against a wall? If they do, is that what is known as a sales pitch?)

Melrose went on to say, "If it is coming out of the dressing room, then I have some liars in the dressing room. If that's the case, then I am worried about that, but at the same time I can't worry about that. If a guy is a liar, he's a liar. I can't worry about that."

Hmm. So let's see now: Melrose says first of all that I am a liar and have a history of lying. If that suggestion has any validity, then the case should be closed right there. But instead, Melrose goes on to bring up another possibility. Maybe a player did indeed give me the information I reported on television. So perhaps I'm not a spaghetti salesman after all. It is the player who is the spaghetti salesman.

Melrose does not say, "If that's the case, then I rescind all the allegations I made about Al and apologize for doubting his integrity." Rather, he goes on to say that he's worried about having a lying player on his team, but he's not worried about it. I guess that made sense to Melrose, but it didn't make any sense to me.

The newspaper in Tampa's neighbour, St. Petersburg, also got into the act. Melrose said to their reporter, "Canada used to be a country where you couldn't lie. I was brought up in Saskatchewan, and if I had lied, my father would kick my butt. But obviously, that's not the case in Ontario, where you can say anything you want without repercussions. I guess there's not much journalistic integrity anywhere in Canada."

So now, it's not just me. It's every journalist in the entire country. And the possibility of the story being the product of a lying player is no longer mentioned. Apparently, it really wasn't worth worrying about.

Since the story was accurate, I had no intention of backing down. But I was not about to get into a war of words with Melrose. Nothing could be gained by it. I said I was right; he said I wasn't. I'd already made my case on TV, and Milbury had made Melrose's.

I simply said on October 25 that the over-under on Melrose's tenure as coach of the Lightning was November 15. In other words, using November 15 as the most likely date, you could place a bet at even money backing his dismissal before that date or after it.

Melrose was fired on November 14.

But the story didn't die there. It seems that, as I had said, the Tampa front office was in a state of chaos. In early December, the now-unemployed Melrose was a guest on a Toronto radio station, FAN 590, and was asked about his experiences as coach of the Lightning.

"I had guys in Tampa who wanted to run the team, and I wouldn't let them," he said. "I wasn't playing the right guys. I was playing certain guys too much. I wasn't playing other guys enough. Every day was a constant battle. Finally, the guys in charge decided they wanted to coach, and they got rid of me. It obviously wasn't a hockey decision because it's not like they've set the world on fire since they got rid of me. They [the players] have got guys in charge that let them do what they want, and obviously that isn't working out very well, either."

Even though he was on the aptly named FAN 590, Melrose was asked to be a bit more specific. Who was he referring to when he said he encountered interference from above? There were two owners of the Lightning at the time. One was Len Barrie; the other was Oren

Koules. Melrose's response was that he liked Koules but didn't want to talk about Barrie.

"They gave me a chance to coach, and I will always appreciate that," he said. "But like I said, I hope Oren Koules does well. I like Oren."

Melrose was not about to forgive and forget entirely, though, Koules or no Koules. "I hope Tampa Bay doesn't win a game in the next year," he added.

So let's do a little detective work here—nothing too demanding, just a little observation and deduction. Melrose says someone above him interfered. There are two owners and he stresses that he liked one but won't talk about the other. So can we deduce which one interfered? I think so.

Discussing "the guys in charge," by which he clearly means Len Barrie, he talks about the fact that they "wanted to coach" and "wanted to run the team." Isn't that pretty much what I said?

But an impartial observer might say, "Wait a minute. It didn't have to be an owner who interfered. It could have been the general manager." It could have been, except for one small problem. At the time that the incident occurred, the Lightning didn't have a general manager. Len Barrie was acting in that role.

Did Barrie interfere as I had suggested on *Hot Stove*? Barrie says he didn't. But he did concede that he had felt Melrose should be making more use of Steven Stamkos, who was a rookie at the time. He insisted that under no circumstances did he tell Melrose to give Stamkos more playing time. Then he added, "But I did say, 'Why not try Steven Stamkos on the point? The kid has done it and played well back there [in junior hockey].'"

Well, that doesn't count as interference, does it? Only someone who is being incredibly picky would think that telling a coach to give a player more time on the power play counts as telling the coach to give him more playing time.

Discussing the matter on XM Radio, Barrie said more. "I told Barry Melrose about five or six things in the whole eight weeks he was there and he didn't listen to me. Maybe Barry should have listened every once in a while because he lost the team fast. Go ask the players, don't sit here and ask me. My thing is that you're paid to do a job, and he didn't do it from day one. How he came in and prepared for this job was total negligence."

How are we doing so far? Have we established the fact that Barrie got involved in the running of the team? Even though he did not publicly admit, as I had said on TV, that he had told players what they should be doing in odd-man situations, is it hard to believe that he would have no qualms about doing so?

Later on, Barry Melrose wrote a book, *Dropping the Gloves*, in which he discussed his time in Tampa Bay. He talked about the relationship between owners and players and said what everyone in hockey knows. If those relationships become too close, they create a volatile situation. Even if the player is diplomatic enough to avoid mentioning his views of the coach, the coach doesn't know that. He worries about it and his view of the player becomes clouded, perhaps distorted.

"Tampa Bay was an impossible scenario for a coach," Melrose wrote. "The players knew it was a screwed-up situation, and I knew it was a screwed-up situation. The owners knew I wasn't going to change, and I knew they weren't going to change. After a short period of time, they decided I wasn't the type of guy they wanted to run their team. I think they consulted with the players. The players didn't really like the way I was doing things, either, so it was an easy thing for them to let me go."

So finally, it all comes out. As even Melrose admits, Barrie was indeed interfering with the relationship between the coach and his players. Take my word for it: this is not the normal way a properly run National Hockey League team operates, to put it mildly.

The Lightning were indeed, as Melrose puts it, "a screwed-up situation." It's a different phrasing than I used on *Hot Stove*, but our messages were identical. Finally, Melrose believes that the owners "consulted with the players." And if the owners consulted with the players, isn't it likely that those consultations would have centred on the two circumstances that are most likely to affect the outcome of any game? Would they not be penalty killing and power play?

We can't always say all that we know, or how we know it. And we certainly can't say it all in thirty seconds on the air. I hope most viewers knew and appreciated that, because a lot of owners and management people certainly didn't. Could I have been wrong? Sure, you can never be 100 percent on some things. But I'm confident that in this case I was accurate.

Part of doing the job means that you're going to annoy people who don't want certain things known. For me, the story wasn't over yet. Pierre LeBrun, who was on the panel that night with Milbury and me, was fairly close to Oren Koules. The segment had hardly finished when Pierre's phone rang. It was Koules, and he wasn't happy. Get in line, Oren. I'm not sure about this, but I think Koules also called Scott Moore, the head of CBC sports at the time, to complain.

The next day, Bill Houston, author of the "Truth and Rumours" column in the *Globe and Mail*, called me. He wasn't questioning the accuracy of the report (for a change), but he was certainly aware that my allegation was causing a fuss. I told him that our job on *Hot Stove* was to unearth the gossip that was making the rounds in the NHL and to pass it along to the viewers. Houston put that in his column, too.

As soon as Houston's column appeared, I got a phone call from Moore. He seemed somewhat upset about the content of the segment on Saturday night—perhaps at the prompting of Koules. But what angered him more, he said, was the fact that I had told Houston that *Hot Stove* deals with rumours and gossip.

"There is no gossip on the CBC," he growled in what wasn't exactly a shout, but wasn't a friendly tone of voice, either. "That's what makes me the most angry. You should never imply that we allow any gossip on the network. The CBC deals only in facts, not gossip."

As someone who had been doing *Hot Stove* for at least a decade before Moore showed up on the scene, I knew that this was certainly not the case. And frankly, for *Hot Stove*, it was never intended to be the case. But Moore didn't seem to be in the mood for a discussion on either the history of the show or the vision created by John Shannon, so I just accepted his abuse for a bit longer until he ended the call.

At that time, all the *Hot Stove* segments were available on the CBC website, so when I got home, I called up the site to take another look at the segment and see if I'd said anything that was really out of order. The show was one of the options presented when the site opened, and the CBC had been good enough to provide a description of what a viewer should expect. *Satellite Hot Stove*, the CBC said, dealt with "rumours and gossip." I guess Scott Moore skipped that session in his History of the CBC indoctrination class.

That was my first serious interaction with Moore, and I think it's safe to say he didn't find me sufficiently subservient. We never did hit it off, and unfortunately he had a lot more clout than I could counter.

To sum it all up, I broke a story that was immediately, and publicly, criticized by Milbury. Barry Melrose criticized my integrity and reputation in two Florida newspapers, and presumably on a number of other media outlets.

The head of CBC Sports made it clear that he doubted the accuracy of the story and gave me a black mark in his mental staff evaluation portfolio. He was angered by my use of CBC airtime to spread rumours and gossip. He gave no thought to the possibility that the story might technically have qualified as gossip but it wasn't a rumour. It was true. And ignored entirely the fact that rumour and gossip were a core part of the show to begin with.

And the public? They probably heard all the fuss and all the denials and thought, "There he goes again. Another one of those crazy stories that they make up on *Satellite Hot Stove*."

Barry Melrose's reaction to the revelations about his team serves as a good example of why people might conclude that the stories we broke on *Hot Stove* were sometimes inaccurate. Melrose's first response to the story was a pretty standard one. He said I had a reputation for airing stories that proved to have no basis in fact. To be precise, what he said was, "Al thrives on BS."

Had he said that to me in person, I would have asked the same question I always asked when people made that type of accusation: "Such as?" No one ever had a decent answer to that. Someone might say, "Well, there have been lots of them, but I can't think of one right now." If they did manage to think of one example, they invariably either had not understood what I had said, or hadn't heard about subsequent events that supported what I had said.

Our record for accuracy on that show—and I'm talking about all the major participants—was very high. According to John Shannon, who received all the mail and fielded all the telephone complaints, the average for each of us was just one bad story per year. In 2009, the year before I left, I tracked all the main stories I'd broken in the course of the entire season and only one had not come to pass, even though many of them had been denied, ridiculed, questioned, or all of the above. I had hit the one-per-year average right on the nose.

And here, I'm talking about the information I presented as news. If I hadn't been able to confirm something, I would say, "This is a rumour that's going around. I can't say it's a fact, but I can say that it's a rumour in the hockey world."

Sometimes, the problem with the stories presented as news was that we were too far ahead of the rest of the media. I once said, for instance, that Martin Brodeur had already signed a new contract with the New Jersey Devils, but general manager Lou Lamoriello was keeping it in a drawer and waiting for a suitable time to make it public. I also quoted the salary Brodeur would receive. When there was still no news of a Brodeur contract after a month, Bill Houston ridiculed the story in the *Globe and Mail*. When Lamoriello finally announced the new Brodeur contract a month later—at the salary I had mentioned—there was no retraction in the *Globe*.

On another occasion, I said on *Hot Stove* that the Montreal Canadiens had tried to acquire Vincent Lecavalier from the Tampa Bay Lightning. Two American writers at the *Montreal Gazette*, Pat

Hickey and Jack Todd, were vicious in their attacks and threw out the usual charges of fabrication. Some months later, Montreal general manager Bob Gainey admitted that he had tried to make a deal for Lecavalier. Former Lightning GM Brian Lawton confirmed it. Not a peep from the *Gazette*'s dynamic duo, neither of whom has a reputation for breaking news stories of any consequence.

And of course, there was the story of the trade of Wayne Gretzky from the Los Angeles Kings to the St. Louis Blues. I was about two months ahead of the pack on that one. In fact, even the upper-echelon managers at the *Toronto Sun* were getting concerned. They had given the original story big play and had been waiting for weeks for it to come to fruition.

I could go on and provide a long list of similar occurrences, but I think the point has been made. Newton's third law of motion also applies to journalism: for every action, there is an equal and opposite reaction.

In all three of those cases, the original report was accurate. In all three of those cases, there was public denial and criticism. People tend to remember the criticism and denial. It is a normal human response.

It is also an inescapable fact that journalists don't like to get beaten on stories, especially when it involves the team they cover and comes from someone based in a different city. When that happens, they have two choices. They can admit that maybe they slipped up, or they can attack the accuracy of the story and the credibility of its creator.

What we tried to do on *Hot Stove* was tell the viewers what hockey people were talking about. If you include players, coaches, scouts, management, and on-ice officials in that group, that's about a thousand people. Sometimes the predictions they made didn't come to pass. But if you're talking to a Pittsburgh Penguins player, for instance, and he says, "All the guys think we're trying to trade for a high-level forward," what should you do with that information?

What I did with it was pass it along on *Hot Stove*. I'd say, "The Penguins think their GM is trying to get a high-level forward." When it didn't happen, we were the ones who got blamed, not the general manager who couldn't get the deal he wanted. And the people who said we couldn't be believed had another piece of ammunition. But what we had said was true. It just hadn't been taken to the next step.

I once reported that the Vancouver Canucks were targeting Michael Ryder, because all their research showed that as a right-hand shot, he would be perfect on a line with Henrik and Daniel Sedin. In fact, I said it more than once. There was no doubt it was true. General manager Mike Gillis will confirm it if you ask him. He and his scouts and the rest of the staff agreed that Ryder was a player they wanted. But when it was time to pursue the deal, they had a meeting where Gillis pointed out that even though they all agreed Ryder was the perfect acquisition, his salary was such that it would prevent the acquisition of other players. Did they still want him? They decided they did not. Ryder did not go to Vancouver, and again, a casual viewer might say, "There's another one wrong for *Hot Stove*."

All of this begs the question, how did we come by our information? Take my word for it, the regulars on the panel knew what was happening in the hockey world. We had virtually no life outside of hockey. We lived in a world that required us to be on the road for most of our children's birthday parties. My own sons were born in mid-April and early June. Since I didn't cover any specific team, I was invariably chasing playoff stories when they were blowing out candles on their cakes. We were rarely home for Thanksgiving because the NHL season was just getting under way. Important New Year's Eve games in a distant city were common. The chance of having a meal with the family without being interrupted by a phone call were about fifty-fifty. This was the era before cell phones, so you got up from your dinner and talked to the coach, GM, or player who was calling. Then you went back to eat the rest of your cold meal while the kids ate dessert and your wife gave you looks that were even colder. We couldn't commit to being hockey coaches for the kids or enrolling ourselves in a university course, or even a bridge club. We would be away too often, especially in the spring.

Eric Duhatschek managed to get away with coaching kids'

hockey—to a degree. He helped the head coach who could actually be there every week. Eric certainly couldn't. But Eric covered a specific team—the Calgary Flames—so he had a lot of home games, and he knew his schedule before the season started. I, on the other hand, was an NHL columnist. I went where stories were breaking, so I had no home team to provide me with a clear-cut travel schedule for the upcoming year and no way of knowing when I would be heading for the airport.

And since I promised to be fully open about this, it's not uncommon for the job to cost you your marriage. When you're away, your wife runs the house. She must. When you come back, you want to be in charge. But she, rightfully, thinks that it was all rolling along pretty well under her direction, thank you very much.

My wife remains a very good friend, but we agreed in 1996 that it was time for us to head down our separate paths. And hers didn't include a devotion to hockey. She still edits everything I write, including this, but when we got married, I was not a hockey writer. The job changes everybody's perspective and priorities.

When we discussed this chapter, she said, "Being married to a hockey writer cured me of being a hockey fan. I never watch games anymore, even though some are available. If you'd told the eight-year-old me that this would happen, I would have said: 'No way.'"

It is not my intention to whine here. I chose this path, and followed it. I'm just explaining. And please don't think I was any different than the others. As John Davidson had been known to say, "I'm a hockey lifer." I'm not now; but I was then.

After the marital split, I lived in a fourplex owned by a high-profile hockey agent. He lived in one unit, and most of the time, the remaining two units were rented to Toronto Maple Leafs players. There was a communal front porch, and in the good weather, we'd sit out there and chat. In the bad weather we'd wander two blocks—or stagger through deep snow before the mayor called in the army—down to the Madison Pub.

Normally, after a game in Toronto, I went for drinks with a player, or a number of players, as often as not from the visiting team. When I was on the road, arrangements were made to socialize with players from one team or the other—usually not both.

It was always important to know the players' favourite places because in the NHL, gossip is the universal currency, and the players, like everyone else, tend to say things after a few drinks that they might not say earlier in the evening. I wanted to be there when they said it.

The on-ice officials are also a fount of information. They hear all kinds of interesting gossip out on the ice when the players start chirping with each other—which is most of the time. One Sunday night in Winnipeg, I was talking to a referee after a game and he said, "Are you going out?"

"In Winnipeg on a Sunday?" I asked, rolling my eyes.

It turned out that he knew what he alleged was a decent place, not one of the usual haunts, and had been assured that it would be open. I said I had to drop off some stuff at my hotel, and I'd meet him there. Why I went to the hotel, I do not know. I'm convinced it almost cost me my life.

I tried to get a cab outside the hotel, which was at Portage and Main, the major intersection in Winnipeg. But it was Sunday night. No cabs. So I started to walk, thinking I'd flag one down. Still no cabs.

Well, if I saw a bus, and I was near a stop at the time, I could get on and warm up. Did I mention it was about 30-below and windy? But no buses. Okay, I thought, I'll stop in a McDonald's or a coffee shop. Except they were all closed.

I am not lying when I say I have never been so cold in my life. I genuinely thought I was in danger of freezing to death. I kept thinking of those World War II films on the History Channel showing German soldiers frozen solid outside Stalingrad in the Russian winter. It is a documented fact that of all the cities in the world with a population of more than 600,000, Winnipeg is the coldest.

I briefly stopped in a doorway to get out of the bone-chilling wind but realized that avoiding the wind didn't raise the ambient temperature. I still needed to move on. Finally, I saw the place I was heading for and staggered into it. I would have sprinted except my limbs were frozen.

The point I'm trying to make is that we even put our lives on the line for this job. We never did so intentionally, but it was the reality. Doug Gilbert, a sports columnist at the *Montreal Gazette* when I worked there, was hit by a car and killed while on the job.

The place in Winnipeg turned out to be a pleasant spot, and I think the referee even bought the drinks. My usual rule of thumb was that I'd buy for linesmen; referees could buy for me. Referees made more than I did. Linesmen made less.

I ran into a veteran linesman in 2019, and he welcomed me warmly. "Remember that night in the Sherlock Holmes in Edmonton?" he said and laughed. "You bought all the drinks and said, 'Don't worry. I'm on an expense account, and I work for the sixth-richest guy in Canada. I'm determined to make him the seventh-richest.' I never forgot that line." That is indeed a line I was known to use.

I rarely had to buy when Canadian players were involved, though. After a St. Louis Blues game in Toronto once, Al MacInnis suggested we should meet at the Madison—a good idea since I frequented the place pretty well every night. I was delayed for some reason, and by the time I got there, Al had been waiting for about half an hour. I apologized, but he shrugged it off. He had enjoyed talking to the three or four other regulars who were settled in at our usual spot at the horseshoe bar. When the evening concluded, Al not only picked up my tab, he paid for all the other guys he'd been chatting with—and some of them had been there watching the entire hockey game.

There were regular spots all around the league where hockey players would gather. There was no permanence in this. A place could be popular for two or three years, then a different watering hole was established.

There were exceptions. In Los Angeles, for instance, the Melody Bar has been known for decades as the place to go if you want to find on-ice officials. Harry O's was more of a players' haunt since it was partly owned by Billy Harris, a former New York Islander.

The Madison reigned as Toronto's prime hockey bar for years, especially when Wendel Clark lived in one of the four units in our place on Madison Avenue. But now it caters more to the college crowd, being on the fringes of the University of Toronto.

My working day usually extended into the wee hours. I say that partly facetiously, of course. Standing at a bar having drinks with hockey people doesn't seem to be an overly demanding part of a working day. And it isn't. It had a very high fun quotient. But the point is that I had virtually no life outside hockey.

I wouldn't dream of going right home after a hockey game. Even though the columns—one during the game and another with postgame quotes—had been written and filed, there was still a lot more "work" to do. There was so much inside information available at sessions in a pub that it was hard to remember it all. And we all approached the job in pretty much the same manner. One of our regular *Hot Stove* panelists had the habit of intermittently sneaking off for a moment or two and surreptitiously writing down information he'd just picked up over the last thirty minutes or so, just to make sure he could remind himself of it in the morning.

Neither of us would ever use that information without doing a further check. If a hockey player told you something in a bar, you went back to him in a more sober moment—or phoned him if his team had moved on—and reminded him of what he'd said. He could then select one of three options: first, on no account was the information to be made public; second, it could be made public but it was not to be attributed ("You didn't get it from me"); or third, it could be used with attribution.

Most items fell into the second category. The third-option items went into newspaper columns, or were aired on *Hot Stove*, or both. But even though a player had said I could use his name, I often didn't. Obviously, the item was accurate if he was willing to be quoted publicly, so why expose him as a source? Teams have been known to crack down on players they perceive as being too friendly with the media, even if their comments do no harm.

Gary Suter used to be a great quote machine when he was with the Calgary Flames. He was proud of it. He even admitted once, "I knew you guys would be asking me about this today and I was awake half the night thinking up good lines for you."

Suter never said anything derogatory, but his quotes were pointed, thoughtful, and often funny. Even so, Flames management called him in and told him to go back to providing opinions more along the lines of "we're all giving 110 percent."

Other items that players passed along to us for the do-not-publish category were used in a different—and extremely valuable—way. In the next city you visited, you could now take that information to a player of your acquaintance and say, "Did you know . . . ?" He probably didn't, so you would pass along the whole story, complete with background—except, of course, the name of the person who told you. At that point, he was likely to reply, "That's interesting. I heard something good the other day, too. Did you know that . . . ?"

Bingo!

There were players on every team who loved to share information, and most fans had no idea who they were. I certainly never revealed sources, but I suppose I can now say that one was Brad McCrimmon. When he was on the ice, no one came close to the net without paying a price—a painful price. He was one of the most popular teammates in hockey, a true stand-up guy—a foxhole guy, in other words. But his opponents tended not to like him much.

We would spend a fair amount of time together and talk about more than hockey. I thought I'd impress him once by telling him that over the years, the McCrimmon clan was noted for providing the best bagpipe teachers in Scotland. He already knew that. We were talking after a morning skate one day and he said, "I'm going to be on *Sports at 11* on TV tonight."

"I'll watch," I said.

"Don't bother. It will be the dullest ten minutes they ever had on that show. I won't say a thing."

I did watch. And he was right. He was friendly and polite and appeared to be accommodating, because, you know, he was happy to be a part of the Flames family and they were all trying their best and none of them had any problem with the way the team played because the coaches all know what they're doing. And he didn't really know much about personnel moves. Of course not. Why would he? The general manager takes care of that, and there was no question that our GM has done a great job if you look at the guys he has acquired like . . . And so on.

Let me just say that when I asked him questions one on one, those were not the kind of answers I got. But I doubt that if you go back through my columns you'll ever see a quote attributed to Brad McCrimmon. He never told me anything that could be considered pejorative or disparaging about other players, but he did explain what was going on behind the scenes, a view that tends to be withheld by players. The only reason I feel I can reveal him as a source now is that he is no longer with us. He was one of forty-four people killed when the plane chartered by the team he was coaching crashed in Russia in 2011. This guy literally gave his life to hockey.

Brad was one of scores of players who would cooperate with a writer he trusted in a one-on-one situation. It was almost like a spy movie sometimes. "Go stand behind that pillar, and I'll come over in a couple of minutes." Or, "Go out that door and turn right. One block down, there's a coffee shop. I'll meet you there." Or "There's a place I go for breakfast every day. When you get to the back, there's a booth tucked away that you can't see from the front. I'll be there at eight o'clock. If you get there early and they try to stop you, tell them you're there to meet me."

Even Gary Bettman once insisted that we couldn't talk until we got out of sight behind a huge concrete pillar. At least I think he wanted to get out of sight. Perhaps he was considering smacking my head against the cement.

NHL players tend to have dull afternoons if they're on the road. They have a morning skate, then lunch and a nap. But that still leaves a couple of empty hours. A lot of them use that time to get on the phone and talk to friends around the league. Once again, gossip becomes the currency. It's not gossip in the sense of being vindictive or hurtful. It's just the exchange of information about what's going on in their world, which happens to be the National Hockey League.

The people who were regulars on *Hot Stove* were also part of that world. We knew a lot. And although NHL players are, for the most part, a wonderful group of people, we were aware of the few that weren't. We knew which players were loathed by their teammates. We knew the adulterers. We knew who routinely damaged hotel property. We knew who smoked between periods. We knew who cheated at golf. We knew who used steroids. We knew who gambled too much. We knew who had a drinking problem. We even knew the pedophiles.

We knew because we knew the people who knew. One team routinely assigned a detective to do surveillance on any player just acquired in a trade. An official of that team once let me in on the result of one particular investigation: "The detective said that in only two weeks with us, that guy has been involved in every crime in the book except murder and grand larceny."

We knew lots of stories that, lawyers being lawyers, we could never use on television or in newspapers. But we knew. There was never any need to make anything up.

CHAPTER 16

Out on a Limb

We generally had good ratings on *Hot Stove*. Once the show was established, we were usually neck and neck with *Coach's Corner* for Canada's top-rated segment of the week.

Naturally, ratings were higher once the NHL moved into the playoffs, but I've been told that of all the regular-season broadcasts, our biggest *Hot Stove* audience was during the show's first season—on the weekend prior to the trade of Wayne Gretzky from the Los Angeles Kings to the St. Louis Blues.

The show aired on February 24, 1996, almost two months after I had written in the *Toronto Sun* that a Gretzky trade was being formulated, the first mention of such a possibility. By late February, the discussion was percolating energetically, and that Saturday morning, the *Sun* gave major play to a story of mine saying the trade was imminent.

It was inevitable that we would discuss it that night on *Hot Stove* and I was a bit nervous about it. Even though I could always toss in the usual disclaimer that things might still go wrong, I was far, far out on a limb on this one. I had said that Gretzky was going to be traded to St. Louis. Everybody knew I had said it. If the deal were to collapse for some reason, nobody would remember the disclaimer.

Our pre-show chat confirmed the topic was high on the agenda, but no one had bothered to reveal the precise nature of the format.

It was probably set up by Ron, who used to love to try to catch me wrong-footed. I prepared as best I could.

As soon as he completed the opening introductions, Ron said, "Al, you're hot on the Gretzky-to-St.-Louis trade possibility. Here's what [Kings general manager] Sam McMaster has had to say in response to the stuff in your *Sun* article today. He said, 'I have had no conversation with any team about any trade for Wayne Gretzky this year.' This is McMaster quoted last night. He also went on to say, 'I understand that Wayne is a national treasure in Canada but we are not shopping the jewel of the Kings franchise at the moment.'" Just to make sure that the audience had got that right, and to leave no doubt that I was being confronted, the quotes were put up on the screen for everyone to read.

The camera came to John Davidson and me, sitting side by side on-site in Philadelphia. JD looked at me expectantly. Even though Kathy Broderick had urged me to smile more, and I usually tried to follow her instructions, especially as the show was opening, I was stone-faced on this occasion. I'm sure most people in the country expected me to counter McMaster's quotes by saying he was lying. (It is true, after all, that general managers have been known to lie occasionally.) But in this case, McMaster was probably telling the truth—I didn't believe he knew the whole story himself. Even if he wasn't being truthful, I wasn't going to dispute it. I hadn't been expecting such a direct assault and perhaps that's why I wasn't as careful with my pronouns as I should have been. But I put forward my case, even though I should have been a little more careful with the pronouns.

I said, "He's right on all those points. The Kings are not shopping him. However, he [Wayne] is going to ask to be traded, and he will go. He [McMaster] has not had any discussions, no, but the people above him have certainly had a lot of discussions, and that's what's going on. The upper echelon of the St. Louis Blues have been talking to the upper echelon of the Los Angeles Kings much further up than Sam, and the Gretzky part is pretty well set.

"All that they have to negotiate now is who goes with him—they'd like to get Marty McSorley in St. Louis and failing that, they would gladly accept Tony Granato or Rick Tocchet—and then who goes back in return? But the deal as far as the Kings' sending Gretzky there is pretty well done. He'll earn $9 million U.S. a year for two years if he goes, as long as the other guys can be worked out. I would say it's ninety percent done."

I don't know if Ron thought I had just been guessing, or making up the story. But I wouldn't make up a story, and, if I did, I wouldn't put a player with as high a profile as Gretzky's in the middle of it.

The NHL has some fairly strict rules regarding management from one team discussing the availability of a player from another team, even when using a third party as an intermediary and even if the player himself has expressed a desire for a move. One of the most infamous cases in that regard involved Alexander Mogilny, who was playing for the Buffalo Sabres at the time. Almo was a true free spirit who said he played hockey only because he needed to do so to support his lifestyle, not because he loved the game. After a while in the NHL, he decided that the Buffalo winters were far too similar to those he had endured growing up in Moscow—and before that, nine time zones east of Moscow.

When the Sabres were about to embark on a road trip, Mogilny announced that he had a morbid fear of flying. He couldn't do it, he said, and from now on, he would play only home games and those he could get to by road. The rest of the Sabres boarded their plane and went on their way. Not long afterwards, Mogilny went to the airport and got on a plane for New York. Once there, he headed downtown and walked into the office of Neil Smith, the general manager of the New York Rangers at the time, and announced his desire to play for the Rangers.

Smith, of whom it was once said by an NHL owner, he "had an unlimited budget and overspent it," screamed in horror at the thought of what would happen if anyone in the NHL's head office a few blocks away found out about Mogilny's visit. Big budget or not, he had no intention of donating a significant part of it to the NHL via a fine and told Mogilny to get as far away as possible and as quickly as possible.

Realizing that he had to wait for the Sabres to trade him, Mogilny suddenly lost his fear of flying and patiently put in five years before the Sabres sent him to Vancouver, a city much more suited to his approach to life. The fact that the Canucks annually logged more air miles than any other team in the league no longer bothered Almo.

John Davidson always knew a lot about what was happening in the league, so after I finished my explanation of McMaster's statements, he said, "Al, what about the idea, though? Next week, there's a meeting scheduled early in the week in Los Angeles, with the management—the ownership, make that, not management—the ownership of the Kings along with Michael Barnett, the agent for Wayne, plus Wayne. Is that just a formality or is that going to chart a new course?" This was JD, who was always supportive, trying to provide me with an out, just in case the trade, which was so close to fruition, somehow went on the rocks.

"They have to work out how it's going to be done," I said. "It's very important to the Los Angeles Kings that, as Sam says, they not be seen to be shopping this guy around. It's important that when it all comes out, Gretzky is the one who says, 'Yes, I was the one who asked for this trade. The Kings tried to keep me, etc.,' because they have to sell some tickets. The Kings then have to make the smart marketing move and say, 'We're bringing in all these kids. We're going to keep Robbie Blake. We're going to keep [Vitali] Yachmenev. We've got a kid by the name of Pavel Rosa in the juniors, another good kid, and were going to build around that with all these youngsters we're getting, so be happy. We've got two young goaltenders in [Byron] Dafoe and [Jamie] Storr. This is the nucleus of a team here.'"

We continued to discuss the deal a bit more, but we had already covered all the essential points, and I thought I had come out of it pretty well.

At the time, my wife and I were in the market for a house. As I mentioned earlier, she and I had agreed to go our separate ways. We were going to live apart, but we would remain friends and we both wanted what was best for our sons. The plan was that they were going to live with her, and I would visit as often as possible, so a suitable house was needed.

Following the afternoon taping of *Hot Stove* and the Gretzky discussion, we drove to the Kingston area, where some of her relatives lived, planning to look at some houses the next day. It was about midnight and we were asleep when the phone rang in our motel room. "It's done," I was told. And there is no doubt that this was a person who knew it to be a fact.

I called the *Sun* and dictated a story. Although the deal had yet to be filed with the league, the negotiations appeared to be complete. Gretzky would go to St. Louis. In exchange, Patrice Tardif, Roman Vopat, Craig Johnson, and a 1997 first-round draft pick would go to the Kings.

On Sunday, we looked at houses near Kingston and even put in an offer on one. In a free moment, I called Gretzky. "Go to Winnipeg," he said. "We're playing there tomorrow night. There are still some parts to be arranged."

Off to Winnipeg I went, and when I met him in the dressing room after the game, Wayne did something he had never done before. He told the rest of the media, "I'll be back." Then he said to me, "Let's go outside."

We left the dressing room and went to the players' bench. The arena was virtually empty by then so he walked down to the far end and signaled to those who followed that they should not come into the bench area.

He filled me in on a few of the aspects of the negotiations, then said, "I'm not going on with the Kings to Tampa. I'm going home. You should go to Vancouver. Are you going to stay at the Bayshore as usual?"

I assured him that I would. That was where I always stayed in Vancouver, and that city was the site of the Blues' next game. "I'll call you there in the afternoon," he said.

The next day, the deal was officially announced by the two teams. By that time, a fifth-round draft pick had been added. McMaster, having read the details of the trade in the Sunday *Sun*, didn't like the fact that the article was totally accurate, so he demanded that a second draft pick be incorporated, just to make the *Sun* story wrong. He wanted a fourth-rounder, but Mike Keenan, GM of the Blues, refused to go higher than a fifth-rounder and McMaster begrudgingly conceded. So when you read details of the trade now, you'll see that it involves two draft picks rather than one, which was the original deal.

Sure enough, while I was in Vancouver, Wayne called and filled in all the details. His unhappiness with the Kings had been focused on the team's refusal to add some quality players and increase the payroll. He had been promised in August that the team would address this, but when they hadn't done it by January, he started agitating for a trade. He felt that he had done his bit to help the Kings' financial situation by deferring part of his salary. But the team hadn't lived up to its obligations.

"I deferred close to seventy percent of my salary," he told me. "Here's a guy [Kings owner Philip Anschutz] who just got a cheque for $1 billion [in a Los Angeles land deal], who paid $115 million for the franchise, and who's talking about a new stadium for $250 million, and he asks me to defer my money. I said, 'No problem,' and I did it. For people to say [the trade] was just over money, it was ridiculous. That part hurt me the most."

The next afternoon, he called again. "You want to go for a sandwich?" he asked. As my waistline testifies, I rarely turn down food. I think there's an obligation of that nature written somewhere in the sportswriter's official code of conduct. This was just a social occasion, not work, so we chatted about a number of NHL developments, exchanged family news, and passed along bits of gossip. At one point, I said, "Other than me, who did you call yesterday?"

He said he had called the hockey writers at the *Globe and Mail*, the *Toronto Star*, and *USA Today*.

"Did you call Scott Taylor?" I asked.

"Who's Scott Taylor?"

"He's the hockey writer at the *Winnipeg Free Press*. He had a column full of quotes from you. He says he called you at your Beverly Hills home."

Gretzky chuckled. "I don't know him. I guess he must have called the Beverly Hills Gretzkys. I live in Encino."

In 2005, Taylor left the *Free Press* amid a number of allegations of plagiarism; some of those writings were shown to be taken word for word from other sources and reproduced unattributed. Initially, I sympathized with Taylor. I didn't agree with what he had done and his approach was widely known in the business, but he was not a bad human being. In fact, I wouldn't mention his departure here had he not then gone on network television and said that he did nothing that isn't done by just about every sportswriter in Canada. He added that people in the profession who were criticizing him for plagiarism should "look in the mirror."

That angered me and it angered a number of my colleagues. I do know some sportswriters—and radio people, for that matter—who make up stories or indulge in plagiarism. One of the senior New York writers is in that group and enough people in the business are aware of it that despite his best efforts, he's not included in the media wing of the Hockey Hall of Fame. But they are a very small percentage. For all of us to be tarred with the same brush by one of them did not sit well in the hockey-writing community. We have a hard enough time defending ourselves against charges of that nature from the general public without having to do battle against someone in our own profession.

The job that the *Hot Stove* people did was certainly not physically demanding. A quick look at our physiques would prove that. But it was definitely mentally demanding. Just like the people you were reporting on, you had to go out and perform on a regular basis, and that performance was evaluated not only by those who were employing you, but, over the course of the season, by millions upon millions of viewers.

Your credibility was on display every Saturday night and even though people were quick to jump on what they perceived as your mistakes, it was imperative that they believed they were honest mistakes. Scott Taylor's assertions had to be disputed.

CHAPTER 17

The Show Must Go On

Scott Morrison is probably the funniest person I ever met. There have been many people who have made me laugh heartily over the years, but Morrison is the only person who got me laughing so much that I was literally on the floor, incapacitated. My knees would no longer support me.

He was rendering his impression of an older, portly member of the Canadian sportswriting corps, doing the twist, so I can't really give it its due by describing it. Scotty had everyone laughing uproariously, but, since I was the only one on the floor, me more than the others.

To no one's surprise, this took place in a bar. But even so, it was fairly early in the evening. It was Scott's impression of our colleague that got to me, not the alcohol. The occasion was Eric Duhatschek's 1986 stag party and it turned out to be a memorable night, so much so that it is still lauded when a few of the senior sportswriters get together. Invariably, at some point, someone will say, "Remember that night in Calgary when . . ."

The bar in question had been recently opened and was located near the Saddledome in an area that was primarily residential. A little research unearthed the fact that it was a '60s bar, thereby earning itself an automatic AAA grade from the hockey media.

It had yet to establish a following in the neighbourhood, which made it ideal for Eric's stag. And since the Stanley Cup final was under way, every hockey writer worth his salt was in town. We could take over the entire place and sing along with the music.

I use the verb "sing" rather loosely here and "along with" even more loosely. Perhaps the only person who has less musical talent than me is Eric. Regardless, we both like to ignore our shortcomings and join in with the singing. In fairness, I don't remember any great vocal talent being exhibited by any of the others, either, although Morrison was pretty good on the "wee-oohs" when a Beach Boys song came on.

The evening appeared to be winding down when the owner decided that he'd like to spend a little more time in the back room— or somewhere other than his crowded bar—with his barmaid. He then made what may be the worst business decision in the history of Alberta bar-owning. (I remind you of the province in which this occurred to make it clear that it did not take place in Ontario where my own disastrous dabble in bar-owning might have been worse. And I probably should mention that even though I was an idiot for getting involved in the bar business, Morrison was a co-idiot. He invested, too.) The Alberta bar owner approached the obvious ringleader with a proposal.

"Do you guys want to keep going?" he asked.

"Sure," I said.

"Then how about those who aren't staying, leave now, but the people who don't want to leave, give me ten dollars each and you can stay as long as you want and help yourselves at the bar?"

I thought Terry Jones, the famous Edmonton sportswriter, was going to collapse from shock. His nickname was "Large," and it wasn't because we couldn't think of any other words to describe him. His eyes grew wide and he quickly started diving in his pockets for money, an act with which he was notoriously unfamiliar. I was pretty sure he was looking for money. He couldn't have been going for his wallet. He always forgot that.

Morrison was wide-eyed, shaking his head in disbelief.

Eric was saying, "Yes, yes."

Globe and Mail columnist James Christie, a wonderful guy who died in 2019, was assuring everyone that this was a fiscally sound manoeuvre for us, as if we didn't already know.

So the elite of Canada's sportswriting corps, if there is such a thing, stayed until daylight. I don't think it takes an awful lot of imagination to realize that letting that crowd loose in a bar at ten dollars a head was a far-from-profitable venture.

Only one of the guys who bought into the ten-dollar undertaking wasn't a media type. He was a friendly chap who had come in as an unsuspecting patron at some point in the evening and had stayed on, presumably to listen to the '60s music (certainly not for our rendition of it). He told us that he had once been a member of the Cascades, which, I'm sure you know, had a huge hit in 1963 with "Rhythm of the Falling Rain."

At one point, he favoured us with a bit of the chorus from that song—probably the only melodic vocal rendering of the evening—and he offered up some interesting stories about the recording industry. His credentials seemed sound enough and we enjoyed his company. It wasn't until years later that we found out that every member of the Cascades was white. This guy was not.

A set of drums had been left on the small stage. I don't play the drums. They require a little more delicacy than you might think. Some of the guys in our group were on the hefty side and if you get a big guy pounding on them, they will get broken. Leaving them behind was another mistake by the bar owner, but it probably didn't cost too much to fix them.

Eventually, we reached our limit, even though at certain times in the evening it had seemed doubtful that such a possibility existed. We decided that we'd had enough and staggered off. There is something decadent about going home from a bar in the early-morning light— assuming you count nine o'clock as early morning. You pretty well have to rule out attendance at the teams' morning skates and write the proverbial "think piece" later in the day. Much later.

Jim Christie was lucky in that he worked for the *Globe and Mail*, which had no Sunday paper, and since it was now Saturday, he could take the day off. He had just collapsed into bed when his phone rang.

"Hello, dear," said his wife. "Remember how you always said what a pleasant surprise it would be if I just turned up one day when you were on the road and called from the lobby to let you know I'd arrived?"

"Oh my God," thought Jim, envisioning having to explain to his wife, who had just flown from Toronto, that he needed to spend the day in bed. Alone. He told me later that he was in such a state of panic that he wasn't quite sure how he responded. The only thing he remembered with clarity was that his wife had been teasing him a bit. She said she had intended to make the trip but couldn't get a flight. He somehow managed to convince her he was disappointed.

And Eric, the star of the show, didn't get his married life off to the best possible start. His wife-to-be was furious that he hadn't answered his home phone all night. But what could he do? He couldn't leave his own stag party, and there were no cell phones at that time. The bar, by the way, went out of business shortly afterwards.

I mention this story not only to make you aware of the dedication with which we pursued our craft, but to let you know that Scott Morrison and I were the closest of friends for many years. That didn't mean we worried about each other's sensibilities. Far from it. He often called me Cliff, a reference to Cliff Clavin, the know-it-all in *Cheers*. His clear implication was that there might not be a lot of substance in whatever I was prattling on about. The fun fact of it is, Cliff was never wrong; he was just tedious. So, take that for whatever it's worth.

The ribbing didn't stop there (or ever). One day, I was holding court in the *Toronto Sun* office, having just returned from Las Vegas. I was saying that I had experienced a strange weather phenomenon: a hot wind at midnight that made me feel like I was standing in a hair dryer. "What would you know about a hair dryer?" asked Morrison, pretending to shield his eyes from the glare off my dome.

Both of us had long careers on *Hot Stove*. In fact, as I mentioned earlier, he was part of the show's precursor, the Saturday-night updates during the 1994 NHL lockout. "They were airing classic games on Saturday nights," Scotty recalled, "and we would go to the studio and have a discussion based on what was happening with the lockout."

When the lockout ended and John Shannon made *Satellite Hot Stove* the mainstay of the second intermission, Morrison was the sports editor at the *Toronto Sun* and I was the hockey columnist. I found out years later that Shannon had decided against having two people from the same paper on the panel. So, although he never told us, Morrison and I were competing for a spot as a regular.

Scotty lost and, as a result, appeared only sporadically on *Hot Stove* in those days. Our friendship continued unabated. It was one of the few subjects that we never broached. Later on, he appeared with more regularity, and when I started doing research for this book, I asked him if people still talk to him about *Hot Stove*.

"Oh my God, yes," he said. "It was such a popular segment that lots of people still remember it, and they miss it. But I don't know whether a show like that could be brought back or not. Maybe it ran its course because you don't have as many trade rumours anymore, certainly not the way it was back then. The salary cap and the economics of the game have taken away a lot of the type of content we used to have on that show. Back in the day, we'd break a ton of trades, firings, hirings, and stuff like that. You just don't see a lot of that anymore—certainly not in the newspaper industry, anyway.

"The TSN guys like Darren Dreger, Pierre LeBrun, and Bob McKenzie are still very good at it. They work hard at breaking news, the trades, the signings, trying to come up with news. Sportsnet was very good for a while then all of a sudden it felt like it didn't seem that was as much of a priority anymore. Nick Kypreos, until he departed, Elliotte Friedman, and Chris Johnston are all very good. But the volume of smaller items, the gossip and the rumours, has changed because of the new landscape. You could see the changes coming even near the end when we were there. I remember that one year, 2009, we drove to Detroit about three times in the playoffs. We'd leave Toronto in the early afternoon, drive to Detroit, get there in time for dinner, go to the arena, watch two periods, and do the show. Then we'd drive back before the game was over and listen to the third period on the radio. They were being so bloody cheap at that stage; they wouldn't pay for a hotel room."

I was a regular that season and Scotty was on more often than not because he no longer worked at the *Toronto Sun* and had, surprisingly, been let go at Sportsnet. He quickly became a CBC employee and even on days when he wasn't part of the panel, he had been lumbered with an extra job.

"If you remember, I was sort of the coordinator," he said. "I would sit in on the meetings and take notes on everything you guys had, and so it was left to me, in conjunction with you guys, to figure out what our lead story was and what the main ones were we had to get to during the show.

"Then I'd go to Ron MacLean during the second period after he had done *Coach's Corner* and sit with him and sort of tell him everything we had on the agenda, what each guy had. I'd tell him what I thought was the lead item. Nine times out of ten, he'd start the segment with something else. It seems he'd always get to the lead item with about twenty seconds left in the segment and we'd have to gloss over it."

It was my opinion that by that time Ron had lost his interest in following the original pattern for *Satellite Hot Stove*. Shannon had always told him to be a traffic cop—do nothing more than send us in various directions and not get involved himself. As time went on, Ron inserted his own ideas more and more.

"I wouldn't disagree with that," Scotty said. "I think as time marched on, if he wasn't bored with it, he certainly offered a lot more opinion. You see the show now and he's basically a panelist most times. A lot of times, he's bringing in what he thinks."

For Scotty and me, that 2007–08 season was our pinnacle. We were on the panel together most weeks and we thought that we were not only sharing a lot of inside information about the hockey world, we were making a lot of people laugh, too. We tried to get in a few one-liners and worked hard at making the show informative without treating our information with the kind of sombre reverence better suited to political broadcasts.

Every Saturday afternoon, Scott and I would meet in the office of Sherali Najak, the executive producer of *Hockey Night in Canada*. We would make phone calls to people around the league to find out what was going on. We might pursue a story together using different sources or just work on our own. We would discuss how our week had gone and complain about the people (fools, of course) we had to deal with in our regular jobs. He insulted me relentlessly, and I responded in kind. We would recall some of our zanier moments over the years, including the infamous night in Calgary and others of its ilk. We laughed a lot. Then we would try to take that upbeat, positive mood onto the set for our segment.

A lot happens behind the scenes that people are never aware of. In January 1986, Scott's wife, Kathy, had had a seizure, and a small brain tumour was discovered. For a while, the doctors monitored the tumour to see how much it was growing. Eventually, she required radiation and multiple chemotherapy treatments. She also had a couple of surgeries over the years and went to quarterly checkups to make sure the tumour wasn't growing. The checkups were always a tense moment because there was no such thing as a win. All you could hope for was a tie, and never a loss. But the ties kept coming time after time, year after year, so there was hope that maybe a win was a possibility after all.

In the spring of 2008, I was in Sherali's office when Scott came in a bit later than usual. I took one look at him and instead of starting with the usual abusive remark, I said, "What's the matter?"

He said, "Kathy had her test."

I just looked at him. I knew this couldn't be good. There was nothing I could say.

"The doctor said it looks like a field of mushrooms in there."

I started to cry.

"How long?" I managed to ask.

"Maybe six months. Maybe a year."

By this time, we were both weeping uncontrollably. I locked the door to the office and we sat there, both of us sobbing and sobbing. At one point, I think we hugged. Later, we went downstairs to the studio and tried to be informative and witty.

Kathy Morrison died on September 21, 2008.

CHAPTER 18

Arguing as Sport

We had a good time doing *Hot Stove* and I always tried to keep the tone light. I still do whenever I talk about those days or sports in general. But doing a show like that invites criticism. And there is one aspect in particular that was, and still is, the hardest to discuss while keeping a light tone: social media.

For all of us who have commented on the game, shared our opinions (popular or otherwise), and reported something true that someone didn't like (surely, the worst of all sins), we have had to answer for it on social media.

No one involved with *Hot Stove* ever directly offered a serious criticism of my work. As I mentioned earlier, John Shannon once warned me against using the show for personal messages. Kathy Broderick urged me to smile more. But that was it. Joel Darling put forward only the nebulous "different direction" as a reason for not renewing my contract and Scott Moore got upset about a comment I made to a newspaper columnist.

But on social media, there was no shortage of abuse. If you're someone who is not used to it, then it would bother you. Usually, however, you can read between the lines and see that you have done nothing more than upset a fan who believes that the team he fervently supports is better than your portrayal of it. He retaliates by insulting you. It didn't take me long to rationalize the whole social media

161

concept. I just reminded myself that throughout history, anyone with a high profile has had critics. *Hot Stove* had given me a high profile so I had to expect critics. It was that simple.

Back when I was still a regular on *Hot Stove*, a friend of mine had to take a lot of medication to control his physical problems. It was no fault of his own. On one occasion, a bunch of us were out for dinner. He probably had consumed one beer too many—which in his case meant a total of two—for his meds to handle and he suddenly started screaming abuse at me. It had nothing to do with anything said that evening, though—at least I don't think so.

A few days earlier, he and I and several others had been canoeing down a river that, because of the spring runoff, was flowing rapidly. There were two people in each canoe, and my partner, who was well past retirement age but still spry and an experienced paddler, insisted that on such a warm day wearing a life jacket would be too uncomfortable. Because of his experience, he should have known better. But because of his age, I wasn't going to argue with him. We were well ahead of the others when we hit a submerged rock and overturned.

For a little while, I was trapped under the canoe, so I had to dive down before I could come back up. When I finally popped to the surface, my canoe partner was hanging on to an exposed rock about twenty yards to my right. I shouted to ask if he was all right. When he said he was I made no attempt to go to him, which would have been a difficult swim considering how fast the river was flowing. So we just waited for our trailing friends to arrive in their four canoes and ferry us to shore.

The guy who shouted at me in the bar had been in one of the other canoes. Days later, at this dinner, when his medications failed him, he launched into a five-minute profanity-laden tirade calling me cowardly for leaving an old man with no life jacket clinging to a rock. He shouted that I was despicable, a waste of skin, a piece of excrement, unworthy of being given life on this planet, and a few other denunciations of a similar vein. I just sat and looked at him until his wife finally ushered him to another table and the bar staff convinced her to take him home.

The others at my table were astonished that I hadn't responded physically or verbally to the insults. "I could never have sat there like you did," said one. "I can't believe you did that."

"I've heard worse," I said.

When you tell the truth on a show like *Hot Stove*, you delight a lot of people. But you infuriate others—especially those who were negatively affected by the revelation. But even people who have no direct connection to whatever was said can also get enraged. Just being a fan of the team can be enough.

In some cases, the responses can be quite menacing. At least my friend in the bar that night didn't threaten to harm me or my family. And I must say, before I go any further, that he came over to my house the next day to apologize profusely. I thanked him for the sentiment and told him that the incident was forgotten. (It obviously wasn't since I'm writing about it here, but it was sincerely forgiven.)

Criticism isn't new to social media, not by a long shot. In the earlier days of *Hot Stove*, people would send letters via snail mail to the CBC. But those notes weren't as vicious as modern messages now that social media has become an integral part of everyday existence.

And sure, there were some face-to-face incidents, too, as I have pointed out, but not a lot. Sometimes players would get aggressive. "What the fuck did you say that for?" was a standard question. Or an entire team could get upset. In retaliation for some of my observations, everyone on the *Globe and Mail* sports staff was banned from the press facilities at Maple Leaf Gardens for a while. Any one of us who was covering a game had to buy a ticket to the green seats (the paper would have sprung for better seats had any been available), then rent a room at the hotel next door to write and file our postgame copy.

I have also known of players who wanted to respond to criticism in a physical manner, but that never happened to me. There was an occasion when a Maple Leafs player, Jamie Macoun, and a *Toronto Star* columnist crossed paths in an almost empty Maple Leaf Gardens. Macoun, whose physical play had been deemed worthy of ridicule by the columnist, suggested that they settle the matter with fisticuffs. The columnist ran away. After that, Macoun would occasionally sidle over to me in postgame situations and whisper some good insights, rather than offer them up in a scrum situation where the *Star* columnist might hear. "I'll never tell him anything," he said.

That's a pretty extreme case, but the point is that it's harder to give, or receive, criticism face-to-face. And, it was always clear during the *Hot Stove* years that the relationship between the media and the hockey establishment had some degree of accountability. That's not the case in the relationship between the media and the public.

As soon as social media took a real hold in our lives, the abuse, the ridicule, the denigration, and the insults started to pour in. It was much, much more than we ever encountered in the earlier years, either on television or in the dressing rooms. Or in bars. Or in all three combined, for that matter. Nowadays, emboldened by the ability to hide behind a pseudonym, people can be as nasty as they want, without ever having to face a personal response to their criticism.

Social media could have been such a wonderful addition to our lives. It could have prompted the exchange of information. It could have encouraged participation in worthwhile activities. It could have created friendships and promoted worthy causes. Some of those positive attributes were realized—sporadically. But really, what social media does more than anything is allow for the exchange of vitriol. No society in history has ever been so adamant in its demands for tolerance—yet, it seems, no society in history has ever been so intolerant. We are a modern society and have the technology to prove it. But when it comes to social media, the mind-set is positively medieval. Or should I say media-evil?

Suspicion is aroused and someone on Twitter shouts, "Kill the witch. Kill the witch." Moments later, #killthewitch hashtags are springing up all over the site. Backgrounds are hastily researched and alleged witchlike transgressions that occurred twenty-five years ago are being posted and retweeted. Memes appear. Cartoons appear. By the end of the day, the verdict is almost unanimous. The transgressor deserves to be tortured and executed. The Middle Ages are back.

Bring on the Spanish Inquisition. We are repeatedly told by people on social media that we must accept all forms of alternate lifestyles in the name of tolerance. Fine. But anyone who asserts a contrarian opinion is vilified.

One of the most enjoyable aspects of *Hot Stove* was that it provided an opportunity, albeit brief, for discussions, debates, and full-scale arguments. We often didn't agree, but that was one of the show's attractions. Viewers could listen to discussions and decide which view had more merit. There is nothing wrong with a good argument.

Perhaps I should tell you about a close friend with whom I used to argue frequently. We once had a twenty-minute dispute on the meaning of a German phrase. Neither of us speaks German.

We had another lengthy debate, although it probably could also be described as a heated argument, on whether a hydrogen bomb explodes (his view) or implodes (my view). Needless to say, neither of us had ever experienced either circumstance. And we're not really at home in the field of nuclear physics.

One time, my friend and I were ejected from a bar for arguing so violently that the manager was sure it would erupt into fisticuffs. We both calmly tried to explain that there was no chance of that happening, but we got tossed out anyway. Once outside, we quietly discussed where we should go next, then went and continued our sport. Arguing is, after all, a sport.

But these days, it seems, you're not allowed to debate. If you disagree with someone, you immediately get labelled as something— fascist, misogynist, racist, sexist, elitist, or whatever. I've even had my opinions dismissed on the grounds that I'm "an old white man." I apologized and promised to complain to my parents about their timing of my conception and their choice of heritage, but it fell on deaf ears. My opinion was still discounted.

Once a person categorizes you with a suitable label, he assumes he has won the argument and will not condescend to discuss the matter further with whatever despicable form of "ist" he has decided you are. On the other hand, when I disagree with someone, people often ask why I hate him. I don't hate him. I just disagree with him. I think his reasoning is flawed. Really, which one of us is being hateful?

When John Shannon started *Hot Stove*, he wanted to stimulate discussion. You can't do that by having everyone offer wish-washy, motherhood-and-apple-pie opinions that couldn't possibly generate any disagreement. We gladly went along and, in the process, upset a few people, but we never really concerned ourselves much with their reactions. Then, as the years went on, social media became more widespread. We started to realize that no matter what we said, a lot of people wouldn't like it. And most of them couldn't stop writing after they'd made that point. They had to say something derogatory about us as well.

They couldn't just write, "You are wrong in what you say." They had to write, "You are wrong in what you say, you moron."

But we evolved, too. We stopped being bothered by it. We accepted that if you're going to do the job the way we did it, abuse was inevitable.

When this manuscript was sent to the publisher, it came back with a number of suggestions. It was already perfect, of course, but that aside, most of the editor's recommendations were well taken. At this point, he asked, "Can you give some examples of social media hate you or your colleagues received for specific stories you discussed on *Hot Stove*?"

My answer was, "No. I can't." I'm afraid I didn't really pay any attention to the social media hate. It came, but when it did, I just shrugged and went to the next tweet.

CHAPTER 19

The "Team Useless" Grad

I'm sure Mike Milbury doesn't remember the first time he aggravated me. I've never asked him, but I'm sure. It was in 1976 and Team USA was in Providence, Rhode Island, holding its training camp for the upcoming Canada Cup. The level of American hockey proficiency was much lower then, so much so in fact that not all the Team USA members could crack an NHL lineup. In the newspapers, the team was frequently referred to as Team Useless. This was in Canadian newspapers, of course. At least they covered it. To say the tournament received scant coverage in American newspapers would be a gross understatement.

Mike Milbury was on Team USA, and its coach was Lou Nanne. Lou had grown up on the same block as Tony and Phil Esposito in Sault Ste. Marie, Ontario, but had played for American teams throughout his NHL career. Somewhere along the way, he had taken out American citizenship.

When I was sent to cover an event, I would hang out with players as much as possible, not because I was what was known in the trade as a jock sniffer, but because I was there to write about the players. Experience had shown that you can learn a lot more in the bars than in the arenas.

On the second night of camp, the players were getting together for a few beers in a hotel room, so I stopped in. The sportswriters'

167

two favourite beers were available: Free and Free Lite. I was talking to a couple of players when I saw Milbury staring at me. He walked over to Nanne and whispered something in his ear. Nanne looked over at me and nodded.

Not long afterwards, Lou, whom I knew quite well, came over and, in an incredibly tactful and diplomatic way, gave me my marching orders. He didn't say a word about player-reporter protocol; he just invited me to his room for a beer or two. Thinking that he was going to let me in on some inside information, I gladly went. But after a while, Lou realized how tired he was and announced that he needed to go to bed.

Obviously, Milbury had decided that I didn't belong in a players' gathering. He was right, of course. Even though I knew some of the players, I didn't know most of them—including Milbury—and they felt uncomfortable with a newspaper columnist hanging around. As it happened, they had no need to worry about me. I wouldn't have reported anything I heard without getting their permission, but they didn't know that. Nevertheless, Milbury's actions still aggravated me (after all, the beer was free). And it was pretty clear that I would not be welcomed back.

More than thirty years later, when Milbury joined *Hot Stove*, he managed to aggravate me some more. He has a great facility in that regard, as anyone who has watched us together on TV knows. But I have to let you in on a little secret. We weren't as upset with each other on the show as we sometimes appeared to be. It wasn't all an act, but we both knew that people watching panel shows are much more interested in friction than in rapport, so each of us showed that we had learned no lessons from Lou Nanne. We were neither diplomatic nor tactful.

When I meet people who want to talk about life on *Hot Stove*, the conversation eventually turns to the other personalities. The first person they ask about is Don Cherry, even though he never appeared on our show. Then they ask about Mike Milbury. Although most people don't know it, the two are very close. There was a stretch of time when you wouldn't have been able to figure that out by hanging around the *Hot Stove* set. They had a very loud blowup one night, and for about three weeks afterwards, Milbury, who had always spent time with Don in the little room that he and Ron shared, sat out in the common area with the crew. But they're both mercurial people, and they got over it. They go back too far to let a little hockey argument end their relationship.

"He's the godfather to my son Luke," said Milbury when we were chatting in 2019. "Luke's forty-two, so that will tell you how long we go back."

When Don coached the Boston Bruins, Milbury played for him. In fact, if it hadn't been for Don, it's likely that no one in the hockey world would ever have heard of Mike Milbury, for the simple reason that he wouldn't have been part of it. It's one of those quirk-of-fate stories that makes you realize how lives and entire careers can be shaped by the most random of events.

When Don's career as a minor-league player ended, he was living in Rochester, New York. He was unemployed, but when a friend asked him to coach the high school team—for no salary, just the love of the game—he agreed.

A few years later, Don had worked his way up the coaching ranks from high school to the minor leagues and was named the American Hockey League's coach of the year. He was offered the job of coaching the newly formed Washington Capitals, but he knew that as an expansion team, they'd be awful and he wanted no part of it.

Harry Sinden then offered him the job of coaching the Boston Bruins (there were no assistants in those days) and he turned that down, too. He wasn't sure he was ready for it. But after some reflection, he changed his mind and took the job at $40,000 a year.

One of the high school youngsters he had coached was home from college for the summer. He had enrolled at Colgate University and told Don that the hockey team there had a tough defenceman he should consider for the Bruins. His name was Mike Milbury.

By the time the Bruins were holding their pre-camp meeting a few weeks later, Don mentioned to the head scout, John Carlton, that they might want to look at a guy called "Mulberry or something" who played at "Colgate or Cornell." Knowing Don, he might have said, "Coldgate or Cornwell," but he says he didn't. Carlton narrowed down the options, and even though Milbury had not been under consideration, he was added to the bottom of the Bruins' prospects list.

He definitely had his flaws, but he made the most of the opportunity, showing up at the rink at 6:30 a.m. to work on his skating, and following Don's advice to the letter. And he made it to the NHL. Once Milbury had earned a regular job on the Bruins, he bought a house in North Andover, where Cherry also lived. It was a fairly remote suburb, so the two of them ended up driving to the rink together for games and practices.

Milbury laughed when I mentioned that. "I don't know if he told you, but I didn't have any choice. It was not an optional ride to the rink. He wanted me to go with him. It was a little weird for a player to be driving to the rink with a coach."

It was, but it had to be an indication of how much Don liked Mike, didn't it? "He certainly didn't at first," chuckled Milbury. "I mean, you know Don. Think about it. It was an uphill battle."

"Yeah, I know Don," I said. "You were a college grad, strike one. And you're American, strike two."

But even so, Milbury played a rugged game and eventually won Don over to the point that he drove him to the rink. There must have been a reason for that.

"Yeah," said Milbury. "He liked to practice his pregame speeches, and he needed someone to listen to them."

As is often the case in hockey relationships, there can be long intervals between meetings. You can see a guy almost every day, but then the situation changes and you may not meet for years. But the friendship is still there.

While Don was forging a career in Canadian television, Milbury was trying to forge a career in American hockey. Don was far more successful. Milbury didn't do a great job as a coach and made some positively awful decisions when he was general manager of the New York Islanders. That's why he was available for *Hot Stove*.

"I had started working with TSN when I came off the Island," Milbury recalled. "I was all over the place. I was working for NBC, but at that time, all they had was weekend games, so I was working for NESN [New England Sports Network] locally and then TSN."

Then, one day during the playoffs, he had a chance meeting at an airport with Sherali Najak. "He came to me with a proposal," Mike recalled. "I liked TSN. I liked working with James Duthie, but to be able to work on *Hockey Night* and on the *Hot Stove* was a great opportunity. It was going to be fun to see Grapes [Don Cherry] once in a while. He was my first coach and a big part of getting my career started, so that was the genesis of my arrival on *Hot Stove*."

At that point, I was a *Hot Stove* regular. The days of travelling around and not being used some weekends because of logistics were gone. I was living in Toronto and was on the show almost every Saturday, so when Milbury showed up, it seemed like a good idea to find out where we were going to go from there. I knew Milbury well enough to know that he wasn't just going to be a bobbing head, agreeing with everything I said. I also knew that Sherali Najak felt the show had been lacking some spark. That's why he had brought me back.

Mike and I agreed to a Friday-evening meeting at the King Edward Hotel in downtown Toronto, where *Hockey Night* used to billet out-of-town participants like Milbury, Kelly Hrudey, and P. J. Stock. We were both a little wary—Mike more than me I suspect because he had a long, well-documented history of being confrontational with the print media, whereas I was used to shrugging off people like him—but it went well.

And really, as I once discovered to my amazement, you never know what people who hardly know you might think of you. Those of you who have seen *Slap Shot*, the classic hockey movie starring Paul Newman, will remember the ultimate enforcer's enforcer who was brought in to intimidate Newman's team. That was Ogie Ogilthorpe.

He was modelled on Bill "Goldie" Goldthorpe, who, like Ogie, had a massive Afro hairdo and is considered to have been the toughest of the tough in hockey's minor leagues—which were more than tough. They were downright vicious.

"Glad to meet you," said Goldie, sticking out a meaty right hand that had inflicted many a blow on many a face. "I always feel intimidated by you."

Who knew that the fearsome Goldie Goldthorpe had a sense of humour? I certainly hadn't expected it. "Yeah, right." I grinned. "Of course you do."

"I do," he insisted. "I watch you on television and you don't put up with any shit from anybody, and you put down anybody who tries to contradict you." I must confess right here that I probably don't have Goldie's quote exactly right. I was too stunned to have a crystal-clear memory of it. But I have managed to convey the general idea. I have met a lot of guys whom I considered to be intimidating, but I never, even in my most self-deluding moments (of which there are many), put myself in that category. After the Goldie Goldthorpe revelation years before, I learned never to assume what people may think about me.

There was never any chance that Mike and I were going to be singing from the same hymn book when we were on the air. We had different views about the source of news. I was never a player. Mike was. I was never a general manager, although I was offered an American Hockey League GM job once. Mike had been a GM, even if he hadn't been very good at it.

Furthermore, he wasn't known for getting along with the media, generally. On one occasion, when he was coaching the Islanders, he was holding court after the game. Mark Hebscher, a Toronto-area electronic media guy making a rare foray into a postgame scrum, asked a question that, it must be conceded, wasn't very good. I don't remember what it was, but it was along the lines of, "Are you disappointed that your team lost?" Milbury just looked at him. "Somewhere, there's a village that has lost its idiot," he said.

During our conversation at the King Edward, I pointed out that people who answer questions in that fashion tend to always be at odds with the media. "I've had relationships with reporters that dealt with confidential matters," Milbury insisted, "but there are some things that should stay in the room. I always felt it was important to keep the dirty laundry in the backyard and not spread it about." He paused, then added somewhat wistfully, "But it just doesn't happen very often anymore."

In my view, that was a good thing. It appeared that Mike and I were going to have our differences in that regard. And we did. On occasion, I would break some news on the show about something that had happened in a team's dressing room and Mike would say, "A player told you that?" Partly, he was challenging me, which was fine, but I always felt that he was also shocked. It was not the kind of information that Mike Milbury would ever have given to a reporter.

And it was another instance in which I was aggravated by Milbury. No decent reporter is going to tell you his source for a controversial quote, or even narrow it down, so it bugged me that he would ask that question, especially while we were on the air.

But our disputes were minor. In that meeting at the King Edward Hotel—in the bar, of course—we crafted a plan. It wasn't particularly ingenious and it wasn't particularly complex. And there was no need for us to enumerate the points. It was clear that we were in accord. Both of us would be honest, and if we felt the need to be critical of the other, we would feel free to do so. We had to. That was the nature of the business. It was show business. But it had nothing to do with our relationship off the air. It became good and stayed that way.

Mike had been excited to join *Hockey Night in Canada*, a show that had been on Canadian television as long as there had been Canadian television, and had been on Canadian network radio even before that. In 2019, we talked about his situation when he started on *Hot Stove*. "I was living in the Boston area at the time and crafting a new career," he recalled. "My week was working probably a couple of nights at NESN. Either Friday night or Saturday morning early, I'd fly to Toronto. Then when NBC started covering the NHL on the first of January, I'd go to the airport in Toronto and take the first flight Sunday morning to wherever I had to be for NBC.

"I had to be there by ten thirty because those games started around noon. It was a slog. We were doing a show that would take us to a doubleheader, so we wouldn't get back to the hotel room until about one thirty a.m. You just wanted to lie down and go to sleep after that."

Even so, he was enjoying the *Hot Stove* stint. "It was fun," he said. "Grapes and Ron were hanging around, so that was good. The focus the show drew from across Canada made it a neat situation to work in. That was my first impression. It was pretty cool. This was where it all started—in the country where it all started—and it made itself famous."

Like anyone who is honest on television these days (a remarkably rare breed), it was inevitable that Milbury would get himself into hot water. For both of us, midweek howls of indignation from special interest groups or NHL teams were commonplace. But Milbury forgot something he knew from American TV, and soon found out was even more significant on the CBC. "Everybody is coached today to be as politically correct as the times demand," he said.

A certain word was in common usage in the hockey world in those days. It's still used in hockey discussions, but not public discussions. And Milbury's was public. During the show, he suggested the game was getting too soft and referred to it as the "pussification of hockey."

There was sufficient outrage during the week that the next instalment of *Hockey Night in Canada* opened with a speech from a leader of a gay rights group and a discussion of the importance of accepting gays into hockey. Viewers were also told that they must cease using words that might somehow equate feminism and weakness, and that they must never make any implications of that nature. I will go no further on this subject. No good can come of it. But I can't let it go without saying that I am not a great fan of censorship.

As for Mike, he realized that in order to stay employed, he needed to say something expressing his contrition. So he did. Whether he was sincere or not, I don't know. But knowing Mike, I strongly doubt it.

It was fun working with Mike because he was never slow to give his view and he never danced around the subject. When Brian Burke was general manager of the Maple Leafs he made a trade to acquire Phil Kessel, and although public criticism of Burke was a daring move at that time, Milbury pulled no punches. He said the trade had set back the Leafs' development by five years. Fans of the team—and of Kessel—were upset, but Milbury didn't care. That was one time when I wasn't going to argue with him. (I might have added my contribution, which was that if you're looking for an expert on bad trades, who better than Mike?)

But none of his *Hot Stove* controversies came close to matching the infamous "shoe incident." It is still regularly discussed, and clips of it often appear on television. In a 1979 pre-Christmas game in Madison Square Garden, a number of the Boston Bruins went into the stands to get at New York Rangers supporters, and Milbury was forever immortalized in a clip showing him kneeling on a fan and hitting him with his own shoe.

"Really, it doesn't bother me," Mike said, "although there's a lot more of it around Christmastime when it's the anniversary, and it's invariably on for three or four straight days. I do get references to it once in a while [like on *Satellite Hot Stove*, for instance, if I remember rightly] but it is what it is. It was a whole ludicrous situation. They always say I climbed into the stands. I didn't climb into the stands. I walked up the steps."

I know those steps well. In Madison Square Garden, the press box is a row of seats in the middle of the stands, so as the game is ending, veteran sportswriters know enough to jump out of their seats and dash down to the walkway circling the lower-bowl seats. Those prime-revenue seats are emptying by then, so you have to fight the flow and battle your way down to a couple of steps at the end of the visiting team's bench. Once there, you're almost at the visitors' dressing room, but if you don't make a quick start from the press box, you might get blocked by the exiting crowd and not get to the room in time to access the players you need.

"I was the first one off the ice," Mike said, repeating a story he has no doubt told hundreds of times. "I had no idea what was going on. I had left the ice because they were fucking nuts in MSG back then. They would throw batteries at you or bottles or whatever they had.

"We had just won a close game. It was Christmas. We were going home. I was happy, and I was the only one in the locker room. Then Chessie [goaltender Gerry Cheevers] finally came in. I said, 'Chessie what's happening? Where is everybody?' He said, 'There's some sort of beef out there.' I went back and everybody was already in the stands. I went from "Merry Christmas" to "Oh shit." My heart rate went up to I don't know what it was. So I walked up the steps. I didn't climb into the stands. Walking into the stands was an experience; I can tell you that."

I was laughing at the story and said, "Well, I guess it wasn't Chessie's nature to get into something like that. And I suppose it would have been difficult in goalie equipment."

"You had it nailed with the first one," said Mike. Cheevers has his own explanation for his reticence: "I was already on my second beer," he laughed. And by the way, even though the incident is occasionally shown on a loop to give the idea that Milbury used his shoe to hit the fan repeatedly, he hit him only once.

This is a guy who went into the MSG stands to defend his teammates. That was old-time hockey and Mike is an unrepentant old-time hockey guy. He might have used the wrong word as far as CBC executives were concerned, but he had expressed his honest view.

He enjoyed his time on *Hot Stove*, even though he lasted only a couple of years. And he did enjoy seeing Don again on a regular basis. "I wasn't able to spend as much time with him as I would have liked," he said. "He and Ron had their little cubbyhole in that greenroom and nobody wanted to get in his way if he was getting ready. I would see him before the show started. But I always sought him out when I arrived, and then later after the second intermission, we'd usually have a chance to chat."

Milbury eventually left *Hockey Night* for a simple reason. NBC offered him what he conceded was "an obscene amount of money." As of this writing he's a regular on the NBC hockey telecasts and gets a lot of airtime along with other regulars such as Keith Jones and Anson Carter.

"It's much different than *Hot Stove*," Mike explained. "We'll hit a hot button and usually we'll get to some of those things in the pre-game show when we have a little bit more time, but unless there's some breaking news that the producer wants to talk about, we usually just do analysis or a feature or something. It's not nearly as hot as *Hot Stove. Hot Stove* was meant to touch on some topics with strong opinions and to create some controversy, as much as being interesting, and I think we did all that.

"I realized from the day I talked to them that my job was to say it like it was—whatever I thought it was. What I'm supposed to do is take my experiences and use them to craft an opinion about a current player, or play, or general manager, or coach. They were paying me for an opinion and whether I'm right or wrong, and I'm judged to be a jerk or a good guy or a bad guy, it didn't make any difference to me. You need to have a thick crust."

I suggested that he might sometimes have felt uncomfortable on the *Hot Stove* set because he had to talk about players—and not always in a complimentary fashion. Many former players who hold down TV jobs feel a loyalty that prevents them from being critical. It happens in every sport.

"I didn't ever feel uncomfortable," Mike said. "I understand how hard it is to do some of these things. I've had experiences at all levels that have gone well and then not gone very well at all, so I admire the guys who say things and get it right. I understand it. You can't get it right all the time. And I feel for the guys who get it wrong, but that doesn't mean that I don't do my job."

But why does he do it? Why do any of these guys do it—the former players, coaches, and general managers? Milbury qualifies on all three counts. Why don't they just take their money, relax somewhere, and enjoy it?

Mike had a ready answer. "Number one, I had a bunch of kids and they all went to good schools, and my timing was off. As a player, I didn't make a lot of money. As a coach, I didn't make that much money. I saw a stat the other day saying that the lowest-paid GM earns $1.5 million and it goes up to around five or six million. Coaches now are anywhere from a million to seven million. I never saw any of those days, although I was okay compensated as a manager. So I'm doing it, number one, for the money.

"Number two, I like to stay busy and this is a much more palatable schedule that I'm on, now that I'm just working for NBC. We work maybe two days in the middle of the week. It can get crowded on the weekend and sometimes they throw in some other games here and there, but they're pretty good about assignments. So it's two or three days a week. We do get slammed during the playoffs, but once they end, I don't work until October and I get paid throughout the summer, so it's pretty nice."

We went back to talking about *Hot Stove*, which also ended each season with the awarding of the Stanley Cup, but unlike his NBC gig, paid by the show. But we agreed that there's more to it than the money. When you're facing the camera as part of a live show that tests your credibility, your knowledge, and your facility with the language, there's always a mixture of excitement and nervousness, but there's also some eagerness thrown in. You want to prove time after time that you can handle this job. When the floor manager begins his countdown, the feeling is the same whether the salary is large or small.

Mike certainly felt that way. "If we had a couple of topics that were explosive—and we looked for those topics—I always liked to have somebody on with me that I knew the angle he was going to take, then I could get ready for the counterpunch."

Mike's presence resuscitated *Hot Stove*. It had never become boring, but it had lost a lot of its excitement under Joel Darling's administration. Once Mike showed up and we had our weekly battles, the feedback changed. People started taking sides.

It was a lot like a hockey game. At some points you're attacking and firing shot after shot. At other points, you're defending, and trying to stay in the competition. As Mike and I went at each other verbally, the viewers started aligning themselves. We both had our supporters and our detractors—and the show was better for it.

"You had to be ready on that show," Mike said. "You had to be flexible. You had to be alert. You had to be quick and you had to be ready to roll with the punches. It was as animated a show as anything I've ever been a part of."

Unfortunately for Mike, he tried to get similarly animated during his NBC playoff telecast in August 2020. His off-the-cuff remarks upset a lot of people. He and NBC parted ways.

CHAPTER 20

Changing Times

I n 1995, a few weeks after *Hot Stove* had made its first appearance, I was living in the Etobicoke area of Toronto. My neighbour, a young guy of thirty or so, ran a sporting goods store. One day, as he was heading out to his car, he stopped to offer me a gift of some sort. I can't remember what it was, but it had come from what used to be his store. He told me that he had been dabbling in a new business for the past four or five years and, in the process, had made so much money that sporting goods were in his past. He was pretty much a millionaire.

He showed me his new product. It was about the size of a brick and weighed only a little less. It was one of those newfangled mobile phones that allowed you to make a telephone call without being on the end of a cord.

It was also remarkable in that it had a screen (basic LED, of course, so no colour) that would show you the numbers you had punched in to make your call. And its antenna wasn't very big even though the phone would set you back $1,200 or so. I'm not going to give a lesson on cell phone history here, but I do want to stress that if you do not believe that technology has changed exponentially since the year that *Hot Stove* started, just compare that cell phone to the one you're using today.

Today's phones are such fantastic devices that making telephone calls, their original purpose in life, is far down the list of things we use them for. They're cameras, alarm clocks, games, flashlights, televisions, archives, and on and on. I'm not opposed to cell phones, but it seems safe to say that unfortunately, largely because of them, *Hot Stove* in the form that we knew it is dead. It could not be revived today. In the show's heyday, we practiced a form of sports journalism that cell phones seem to have killed, or at least mortally wounded.

Those of us on the *Hot Stove* panel would talk to players and socialize with them. We could get to know them and joke with them. Even the tough guys who frightened their opponents were invariably good company.

When Dave Manson was playing for the Maple Leafs, for instance, he would regularly patronize the Madison Pub after home games, and I'd insult him mercilessly. Even the night he was awarded a silver stick for having played a thousand games, I said, "Just think, Charlie [his universal nickname], if it hadn't been for your suspensions, you'd be getting an award for *two* thousand games."

"That's enough of that, Strach," he croaked, and we went back to our beers. He had once been cross-checked in the throat by Sergio Momesso and his vocal cords had been damaged. He meant to get the matter seen to after his career, but to the surprise of everyone, probably including Charlie, his career ran for sixteen years. By then, the damage was permanent.

We were once discussing his impressive longevity, and I suggested that much of it had to do with his ability to terrify people. He agreed.

"Unfortunately, Charlie," I said, "three of the people you terrified were behind your own bench."

"That's enough of that, Strach."

He'd laugh and we'd return to what is generally known as hockey talk. Having been with a number of teams, Charlie knew players all over the league and had lots of useful information. But today's players don't often hang around in bars with sportswriters. There is too much technology lurking.

For example, these days, a girl can approach an unsuspecting player who is having a quiet beer with friends and plant a kiss on him (needless to say, the sportswriter has nothing to worry about in this regard), while at the same time an accomplice, who had been waiting with her cell phone poised, takes a picture. Within seconds, the picture is around the world on one of the social media outlets. Now the player is in trouble, especially if the girl is underage—and take my word for it, an underage girl in a bar is not unknown, especially in Canada.

Sure, the player can probably—after a lot of anguish—explain it away and convince his wife of his innocence. But the stigma of the original photograph exists all over the world, and it doesn't erase easily. To add to the problem, even sportswriters who should know better immediately start churning out condemnation on Twitter and similar sites. The concept of innocent until proven guilty is not widely practiced on Twitter. All celebrities dread being caught on someone's camera phone in what appears to be a compromising or an unflattering situation (for example, if you trip and fall, you must be drunk). Photos get taken and used out of context.

In England, where a pub visit is a way of life, a few professional soccer players have been goaded into pub fights while the instigator's friend stood by with his smartphone camera. It is all but impossible for celebrities of any sort to go out in public and relax. It is obviously a much larger issue than girls victimizing hockey players, but that's the aspect that most affects *Hot Stove*.

Social media has changed the way news, rumour, and gossip circulate. It certainly happens a lot faster now. But the simple, inescapable fact is that when we were doing that show, lots of players went into lots of bars. And lots of media representatives went with them. I was one of them. Now the players don't go into bars (though, that hasn't stopped me). Even though we had many ways to gather information, conversations in bars over beers (players tended to avoid hard liquor) were always highly productive.

As if the fear of social media notoriety weren't enough, there is another way in which cell phones have altered the interaction between the players and the media—and not for the better. When *Hot Stove* was entering its final years, the NHL's public relations personnel were grappling with a problem: What to do about phone pointers?

These are people who claim to work for some Web page, podcast, blog, or other internet-based activity. They may have a follower or two. There might be a dozen lonely people in isolated communities who read the uninformed drivel these hacks churn out. They may even get themselves a regular spot with a website that pleads for unpaid content and will print any submission, no matter how inane—and no matter how much of it has been "borrowed" from other sources.

When phone pointers first started demanding media accreditation, the league's PR staffs stood firm. They said accreditation was a privilege accorded only to those who would disseminate information to a significant number of people: TV stations, large newspapers, radio stations, and magazines. No one else.

But the blog people insisted that a modern era of journalism had emerged. They, too, had the right to accreditation because even though they had no credible numbers to submit, their work was displayed on the internet. In theory, everyone in the world had access to their offering.

And to be fair, there were some bloggers who had followers and were credible, such as people who dealt with analytics or hockey history. So the PR staff gave them accreditation. That put them on a slippery slope. People who offered mostly opinion but with an occasional fact thrown in demanded equal access. Now, when the dressing room door opens, most of the people who go through it are from the "internet media." And really, in far too many cases, they are nothing more than fans—sports voyeurs who have found a means of getting close to their idols.

As soon as a player emerges from the back room (which is always off-limits) and into the dressing room (where no one actually dresses), these people rush to get in front of all the other phone pointers and record whatever the player says. What they do with the recorded matter, I do not know. But it's my strongly held suspicion that they do little more than show it to their friends and brag about having been in an NHL dressing room.

Even though the dressing room was never exactly a sacred place, guidelines for access were flexible long before phone pointers found their way in. When I started covering the Montreal Canadiens in 1973, the dressing room was where the players actually dressed. The league was about 99 percent Canadian in those days and it was either the "dressing room" or just "the room"—never a locker room. After all, there were no lockers. Until Americans came into the league in force, that term was not used in the NHL.

The players had stalls and hung their street clothes on hooks. After their postgame shower, they got dressed in front of their stalls. (In the Canadiens' room, it took a little longer while the players eased Stanley Cup rings onto their fingers. The accepted method is to lick the fingers first.) On a table in the middle of the room was a galvanized tub filled with ice and bottles of beer (Molson, of course).

About three years later, an exercise room was added and it was ruled to be out of bounds to the media. We moaned loudly (no surprise there), but the Canadiens were steadfast. The beer tub disappeared. (More loud moaning—same result.) The small medical room had always been off-limits, but now the exercise room was off-limits as well.

Over the next few years, new arenas were built all around the league, and instead of having one dressing room, they had a dressing room complex. There were rooms in which the players dressed and undressed; workout facilities; media rooms for watching game films; shower rooms; medical rooms; dry-land training rooms; coaches' rooms; equipment rooms; and finally, oh yes, the "dressing room." It was the only one of all those rooms that was not off-limits to the media. And usually, by the time the media were admitted to it—ten minutes after the final whistle, according to league protocol—there was no one in it.

Nowadays, a horde of media enters an empty room and waits for a team's PR person to drag out someone who may or may not have been noticeable during the game, and has been coerced into answering a few marshmallow questions. For the most part, the players don't mind being there and are happy to carry on cheerfully. But whether they want to continue or not, the PR person will usually allow five or six questions, then announce that the media's time with the player has expired. After all, it would be dangerous to establish a precedent and allow postgame interviews to go on too long. Something worthwhile might be said. The player is then shepherded back to somewhere else in the complex that is out of bounds to the media. We wouldn't want him to somehow sneak in an over-the-limit answer, of course.

In recent years, there has been a further development along the same lines that also makes the acquisition of inside information difficult. In fact, that was the reason for its creation. It's the in-house media person.

All over the league, teams have set up their own Web pages and hired someone to fill them. You can go onto that team's page in the morning and be told which lines and defence pairings the coach used in the morning skate. You can find out which goalie left the ice first and is therefore the probable starter in the evening game. These people are shills. Nothing more.

Far worse, from the independent sportswriter's point of view, is that you can find out everything the coach said after the skate. You can also find out everything that was said in the primary scrum—the one involving the player with the highest profile at that moment.

The in-house media people, who often were genuine reporters before they sold their souls to the dark side, push their way into any quote-producing situation, point their cell phones, record every word, and publish it. A decent journalist, who has studied background material and is planning a feature with lots of insight, discusses it with a player. A few minutes later, he finds all his hard work posted on the team's website.

I can understand the motivation of these team shills. The decline of newspapers resulted in their being made redundant and they have to live. So they go to work for the teams. Nevertheless, by doing so, they make life difficult for the reporters who haven't been made redundant yet—but whose chances of becoming so are increased by the work of the in-house reporter.

When *Hot Stove* was in its heyday, in-house media people (IMP would be an appropriate acronym) did not exist. No team had its own Web page. The coach would be available for a while after the skate. Then most of the media would move on and he would be available for one-on-one questions, or even just a social chat to maintain good relations.

That doesn't happen anymore. The IMP will not leave the coach alone for a second. Every word the coach says, relevant to the public or not, will be posted unfiltered on the team website within a few minutes.

Once the coach is out of the way, the IMP will attach himself to the player attracting the most attention (assuming there's more than one player in the room, which isn't always the case). Again, the blanket coverage will soon appear on the team's website. With so much digital recording taking place, chances of an interesting insight being revealed are slim. No player wants to say something that management might not like. And who knows what that might be? A simple comment like, "We've allowed twelve goals in our last three games," might be seen by management as a criticism of the goaltending, or worse still, management's inability to draft better goalies. So the player says nothing.

I don't mean to suggest that access couldn't be a challenge in the past. The media's right of access to players has been the source of conflict between the NHL and the Professional Hockey Writers Association for as long as I can remember. As in everything else, there are ebbs and flows. Sometimes access was relatively easy. Sometimes it wasn't.

In general, it's safe to say that whatever the status of the battle might have been at any given time, access was always better after a morning skate than after a game. And it was better on the road than at home. NHL players recognize a hierarchy, and they know media faces even if they don't know names. If a player recognizes someone on the road that he regularly sees at his home rink, that person likely gets preferential treatment.

After the morning skate on the road, the room usually wasn't busy because the local media didn't want much from the visiting team before the game. A local guy might come over and point his phone, so you would just glare at him until he had finished asking a question or two and shuffled off. I know I'm not being very charitable here, but to my mind, I had a job to do and a mandate to fulfill. If the guy had a good question to ask (highly unlikely), I wasn't stopping him. But I wasn't about to let him piggyback on my hard-earned information and perhaps make it public before I could.

Another trick was to pick your spots. This worked especially well in the playoffs but was often useful in the regular season as well. I'd wait until the PR person announced that the coach was about to go to the podium. Everyone would rush out of the dressing room. That's when I'd ask to talk to a player I knew well who would come out and give much better stuff than whatever the coach was offering. Furthermore, if it was the playoffs, whatever the coach said would be on the quote sheets distributed by the PR staff in fifteen minutes or so anyway.

Depending on the building, there was another tactic. In Toronto's Scotiabank Arena (formerly the Air Canada Centre), for instance, there is a standard route that the players use to leave the building. I used to hang around about halfway down that route. Before long, someone like Alexander Mogilny would come along and want to talk about Premiership soccer or Tie Domi would walk past and shout that I was an asshole. That sequence of events actually happened, by the way. Almo laughed, shook his head in amazement, and went back to discussing the Premiership. I rolled my eyes. Domi trundled off. Needless to say, Domi wasn't my closest friend on the team. But I got along exceptionally well with most of the Toronto players, and when I was hanging around their exit route after the game, they often stopped to chat.

When we did *Hot Stove*, we got a lot of our information in social circles. But the majority of it came from one-on-one talks after morning skates or after games. Today, thanks in large part to the cascade of phone pointers, some of whom work for the team, one-on-one chats with players and coaches are all but nonexistent. As one hockey agent told me recently, "If a writer wants to spend some time with a player these days, he'd better bring along an Xbox and download Fortnite." Fans might ask why they should care about all this. The answer is that although there is plenty of news about a team or player, it's almost exclusively information the team and the league want you to have. It's all the "give 100 percent" approach, and the "cut down their time and space" strategy, and the "huge" contribution made by every teammate.

You no longer hear of someone like Brett Hull announcing—during a Stanley Cup run, no less—that his team's defensive pairing of Derian Hatcher and Richard Matvichuk clearly deserved the Norris Trophy because night after night they shut down two top lines—"theirs and ours." On another occasion, when told that a teammate had done well on a conditioning test, Hull's lightning-quick response was, "How did he do on the IQ test?" Hockey players have a lot to say. In the past, they were always articulate, insightful, and available. Only the first two remain.

Whether the climate of the day made access easy or difficult, the people on *Hot Stove* knew how to get the players and coaches alone, and therefore how to get to the inside information. I imagine that if *Hot Stove* existed today, it would still be possible to get the nuts and bolts—the trade rumours, the potential rule tinkering, the coaches on the hot seat, etc. But the inside stuff—the on-ice chirps, the love triangles, the pranks, the politically incorrect nicknames, and so on— would be missed. There would be no way to get players alone long enough to get to material of that nature. And so it wouldn't really be *Hot Stove*, would it?

CHAPTER 21

Let's Make a Deal

I have liked Jim Hughson for a long time. I can't really say how long, just that our paths crossed in my early days of covering hockey when he was a Vancouver Canucks broadcaster and we have remained friends ever since. We were on the phone in early 2020, catching up and chatting about the state of the game. "I don't think you would like working your job in the game right now—in terms of having to make contacts and things—because of the players," Hughie said.

In his capacity as the top play-by-play man for *Hockey Night in Canada*, he's a lot more conversant with today's players than I am, so it was worth hearing him out. "I just think it's different now," he said, "but the world is different. The players are just so vastly different than in the past."

Hughie knows how I used to work from when he was a regular part of the *Hot Stove* panel. I would spend a lot of time talking one on one to players. "You very rarely get anybody one on one anymore," Hughie said. "At one time, you could wander into the dressing room after a practice and just spend fifteen or twenty minutes BS'ing with a player about any number of things. Now, if you start to talk, there are five different microphones coming in, and, of course, there's always the team's media guy hanging over the top." There was an element of that in the past, especially in places like Toronto and Montreal. But the player and I could avoid it by going for a beer and discussing matters privately.

"Part of the problem is they don't *want* to go for a beer anymore," Hughson said. "They're just different guys. They take a protein shake and go back to lunch and watch videos and talk to their specialization coach. Some of them are very respectful guys, like [Connor] McDavid and [Auston] Matthews and [Sidney] Crosby. They're very good guys, but they're so controlled and their message is so controlled. That sounds like an old guy bitching, and I hate being that guy, because the fact of the matter is the game is pretty good. It's fast and fun."

In fairness, I should point out that our conversation had started with his observations about his acceptance of today's fast, free-flowing, low-contact game. The stuff about player availability came later when, like the old farts we are, we switched the discussion to the early days of *Hot Stove*.

"A lot of people don't like the way the game is played right now," Hughson said. "I happen to like it. I think it's great, but I don't like to disrespect the way the game has been played over the years. I've accepted analytics, and I've accepted a whole bunch of different things and I've tried to understand it. But it is just a different world. The young guys come up and most of them have an entourage now because they have private consultants. They spend a lot of time with people who help them out. There's so much staff on the teams now with the sports science people and the sports psychology people. I don't think that's a negative comment at all. It's just a fact."

In the days that we were doing *Hot Stove*, Hughie was also the broadcast voice of the Vancouver Canucks. Because I spent a lot of time covering hockey in Western Canada as a newspaper columnist, our paths frequently crossed. When that happened, out of our sense of duty to the local entrepreneurs, we would spend some money in their establishments—until closing time, more often than not.

I thought then, and I think now, that Hughie is Canada's best play-by-play man, even though he's up against much tougher competition now than he was in those earlier days. I had just one niggling complaint about his play-by-play in Vancouver. Admittedly, I had never done his job, but to no one's surprise, I still felt qualified to straighten him out on this matter. We were in Winnipeg and trying to make the two-block dash from the bar back to the hotel before being overcome by hypothermia when I decided to enlighten him.

I said, "You know, Hughie, sometimes you say, 'Teams are at full and even strength.' You shouldn't say that. It's redundant. If they're at full strength, they have to be even, don't they? Full strength means five skaters and a goalie. So if both teams are at full strength and have five skaters and a goalie, then they're even, right? You don't have to say they're at full and even strength. Just say they are at full strength." I should perhaps have mentioned that I had a math minor at university and could therefore work out complex statistical problems of this nature. I was obviously into analytics long before it took hold in the following century.

"I don't say that," Hughie said.

What could I say in response? I guess we could have had a refrain of "Yes you do" and "No I don't" for a while, but there didn't seem much point in it, so we turned our focus back to staying alive and moved on.

That was as much of a dispute as I ever had with Jim Hughson. It was not exactly what you'd call vicious or acrimonious. I mention that because I'm trying to make the point that I like him as a person and have tremendous respect for his ability as a play-by-play man. But he probably shouldn't have been on *Hot Stove*. He was good at his job, but he didn't fit the format. Putting Hughie on that show was like sending a cocker spaniel to a pit bull convention.

Saturday after Saturday, just before 3 p.m., Hughie, JD, and I would get settled into our surroundings, wherever they might be that day. Ron MacLean, pretending as always that there was a chance he would institute some semblance of order into the show, would say, "What have you got, JD?"

JD would reveal whatever insights he'd picked up that week from sucking up to Gary Bettman, although he was careful not to identify his source. Then he might offer a couple of other items that had come his way from a general manager or two. JD always had some nuggets.

Then Ron would say, "What have you got, Al?" And I would tell him what stories I'd heard around the league from players, agents, general managers, on-ice officials, or all of the above.

Then Ron would say, "Hughie?"

"Oh, I'll just pick up on what those guys say."

It was the same every week. If Jim Hughson brought one single piece of breaking news to that show in all the years he did it, I don't remember it. So why was he there? John Shannon explained it to me once.

"We were *Hockey Night in Canada* and we were trying to service different audiences," he said. "You and the other Canadian guys who came in were on the show to cover Eastern Canada. Jimmy [Hughson] was on the show to cover Western Canada. And JD was on the show to cover the United States. We thought we blanketed the National Hockey League."

Shannon's dilemma was that, rightfully enough, he wanted somebody from the west, preferably Vancouver. The only sports columnist of any standing in that city was Tony Gallagher. But Gallagher and I are a lot alike, and Shannon knew that the show wouldn't work with two of the three panelists being whiny, sarcastic, and combative. One was plenty.

Actually, Gallagher did make it onto the show three or four times over the years when Hughson was unavailable, and encountered the usual condescending approach from MacLean. "I remember one night I came with the fact the Canucks had re-signed Marc Crawford as coach to a new three-year contract," Gallagher recalled. "Nobody else had that and if that happened, normally, everyone would call it a scoop and be good with it. But MacLean somehow seemed keen to downplay the story. His response was a casual, 'Well, his team is going well, so yes they're going to re-sign him.' I got the distinct impression he wanted someone else in that seat, but I had no idea who. While it was true that Crawford's team had been going well, a hard cold story that nobody else had was pretty highly valued, I thought."

Gallagher had learned the lesson that everyone else on the show already knew. MacLean's evaluation of the worth of a story invariably differed from the opinion of those who covered hockey on a daily basis.

I don't want to be critical of Hughson, but I do want to take strong exception to one opinion of his: the opinion that sportswriters should not tell their readers, or viewers, what is being said in the hockey world.

Hughie is a congenial guy. He likes to get along with people. He doesn't ever want to go into a dressing room and be accosted by a player who feels that he has been slighted during the *Hockey Night* broadcast. Similarly, he doesn't want to be wandering through a press box and be accosted by a general manager who feels offended by something he might have said about one of his players. That's fine. That makes him a good announcer. But it also made him a relatively poor participant on *Hot Stove*.

To me, and to all those who followed us or joined us on *Hot Stove*—Pierre LeBrun, Eric Duhatschek, Yvon Pedneault, Scott Morrison, and so on—the nature of the job was clear. Break stories. Tell the viewers something they didn't know. Take something that a team had seen as confidential information and make it common knowledge.

And in that regard, nothing got viewers more excited than inside information regarding a possible trade. Providing that kind of excitement was our raison d'être. But Hughie not only avoided stories of that nature, he was outraged that there were so many of them.

Each year the trade deadline was a big part of the show. It still is for every pundit, writer, columnist—you name it. For our first show after the deadline one year, MacLean started by going to Hughson for his take. A pretty rare occurrence, but on this occasion Hughie had decided he wanted to take a stance, and had alerted MacLean before the show. MacLean introduced him and said, "What did you think of the trade deadline?"

"Not very much, quite honestly, and I'm glad it's over," said Hughson as he launched into what was clearly a well-rehearsed sermon. "I hope the program is not any shorter tonight because we can't throw out any trade rumours. I thought it got pretty silly, actually." And he continued.

"The rumours were flying around and if ten percent of the rumoured deals had taken place, ninety percent of the players in this league would have changed teams. The rumours were so crazy as we came up to the trading deadline that I don't think any of them could have even remotely happened. They were just being pulled out of thin air and I think now, with the internet, everybody is just exchanging ideas all over the place and what happened, it seemed to me, was that a whole lot of credible journalists and reporters lowered themselves to a competition to see who could have the craziest deals and I don't think most of them were going to happen."

Wow! Quite a tirade. He had suggested that the sportswriters of the nation were totally devoid of integrity. I dispute that. We do have standards. They may be low, but they are standards. And they're not low enough, with very few exceptions, to make up crazy deals.

This may have been the first time in his *Hot Stove* career that Hughie said anything forceful, but instead of using his newfound fortitude on some failing in the National Hockey League, he decided to mount an attack on the other members of the panel.

It must be conceded that *Hot Stove* had been the source of a fair number of these rumours, so I tried to explain the process that leads to trades in the NHL. I mentioned that a trade is rarely a one-for-one offer that is immediately accepted by another general manager. Usually, what happens is more along these lines. A general manager (lets refer to him as GM1) might be looking for a defenceman. So he calls a GM buddy (GM2) who used to be a teammate back in the good old days (there's a lot of that in the NHL). "Are you thinking of moving Player X?" GM1 asks. "No, but GM3 might have someone who interests you. He called yesterday and said he's got four players he'll move for the right deal." GM2 then rhymes off the names of the four players in question. When GM1 is contacted by a tame reporter a little later, he has no problem revealing the names of the four players GM3 has on the block. The ball is rolling.

Now, although it may be hard to believe, reporters have buddies, too. And the good ones all have tame GMs they can count on to keep them informed. And reporters (usually in different cities) talk to each other often. So now, two reporters exchange names and between them, they know of eight players who are on the block. And those eight names get into the newspapers.

Maybe only one of those players gets traded. More likely, none of them get traded. But those eight names were made public and those players were said to be on the block. So what did we have there? Nothing more than eight unfounded rumours? Or were there some solid stories based on facts? At least eight facts, if you're into analytics.

Should the reporters not expose the names of the players until a trade has been consummated? Somehow, I can't imagine a sports-writer going into his managing editor's office after his local team has announced a deal and saying, "You know, boss, each team had four guys on the block and they finally settled on these two. I knew all the names, but I didn't want to put them in the paper because it might upset my friend Jim Hughson."

Needless to say, I strongly disagreed with Hughson's implication that reporters fabricated stories because they were "lowering them-selves" and making up what he saw as crazy deals.

It was, of course, my contention at the time that the kind of news-paper people who appeared on *Hot Stove* didn't need to make up stories. A much bigger problem was weeding out the stories that were being floated for a reason other than accuracy.

There's no doubt that we got burned once in a while. It was rare, but it happened. I was once told that a certain player was being shopped. For argument's sake, let's call him Brendan Morrison of the Vancouver Canucks.

The story came from two general managers, one in the east and one in the west (who was not with the Canucks). When I passed along the information on *Hot Stove*, Brian Burke, who *was* the GM of the Canucks, flew into one of his characteristic rages and denied the story. There are several possibilities here. They are: (a) Burke was telling the truth; (b) Burke was lying, and trying (as he has been known to do) to deflect attention with bombast; (c) I made it up; (d) the two GMs who despise Burke (and there are more than a few of them) set me up.

I know (a) isn't an overly common occurrence but it does happen. I know better than to suggest it was (b). I also know it wasn't (c) so I lean strongly towards (d). I have spent many an hour leaning on a bar rail with those two GMs, and a "tip" like that is something that would give them great delight. It's a good hockey-style practical joke and it upset Burke. Double delight. They may still chuckle about it.

I talked to one of them not long ago and he suggested that we get together for beers the next time he's in South Florida, where I now spend most of my time. "I'll buy the first forty-eight, then you're on your own after that," he said. After forty-seven, I might be able to get him to tell me the truth about that incident. Better still, I'll get him a couple of black sambucas. That's the one drink he doesn't handle well—and in the process, I'd conform to the usual blueprint for drinks-buying in these circumstances, namely forty-seven on his tab, two on mine.

So, yes, sometimes stories were made up, but not by us. On the other hand, Hughson's approach was simply out of place on *Hot Stove*. There was nothing wrong with how he liked to talk about the game, and his style had its place. But that show wasn't it.

Shannon created *Hot Stove* to reveal what was being said in the hockey world, and the hockey world is full of gossip: some of it unfounded, some of it deadly accurate, but all of it passed from one hockey person to another. Items that Hughson saw as unfounded rumours were the subject of conversations involving hockey people that week, and that's what most of us wanted to pass along to the viewers. It's also what most of our viewers wanted to hear.

When I made that point on the air, Hughson backed off somewhat. "Doubtless there were some legitimate stories about players moving," he conceded, "but it snowballs to the point where it becomes a little bit ridiculous."

We moved on to other topics, but Hughie refused to let the matter die. He came back to the subject of the annual barrage of trade rumours. "So you want to get rid of that?" he asked rhetorically. Wait a minute, Hughie. None of us said we wanted to get rid of that. You did, but you're on a pretty lonely island out there. However, Hughson had a concept he wanted to propose. Clearly this matter had been bothering him for some time and he was determined to be heard.

"Move the trading deadline up," he said. "Teams know by Christmastime or early January what their needs are. Make them make their deals, and at a time when the hockey should be great and the playoff competition is at its hottest, so we can concentrate on hockey instead of all the other stuff that tends to be pretty distracting."

I had some trouble understanding the logic in that. In all my years, I have never seen a game stopped in order to allow fans to be told about a potential trade. If you want to concentrate on hockey, go ahead. Watch the games. No matter when the trade deadline occurs, newspapers are still going to devote space to reporting on results, injuries, slumps, streaks, and all the other aspects that make up the coverage at other stages of the season.

It was Hughson's belief that fans did not treat the regular season with sufficient reverence. He felt that too many fans sloughed off the regular season and adopted the idea that only the playoffs mattered, and other than that, didn't care about their team's spot in the standings. They should appreciate the season more, he said, and not be given the distraction of a trade deadline six weeks before the playoffs started.

Again, he had raised a point that could be the substance of a debate. In my view, he was wrong and I would have no problem taking an opposing view and defending it vehemently, but it was still debatable.

A major objection would be that the Christmas trade deadline that he was proposing ignores the fact that some teams face financial restrictions. In March, such a team might be able to afford to pay the remaining few weeks of salary of a star player who was in the final year of his contract. But at Christmas, it would be a different story. They couldn't afford to pay him for half a season.

Do we want that team to resign themselves to an early playoff exit—if the team even makes the playoffs—because in March they were no longer allowed to trade for a player who could have made a big difference in their Stanley Cup run? Do we want fans to accept there's no hope for improving their team after January?

And what of Hughie's suggestion that fans would pay more attention to regular-season play if there were an earlier trading deadline? If fans believe in January that their team is out of the playoffs, and know the team cannot acquire any help to shore up troublesome areas, they'll pay less attention, not more.

But aside from the idea of moving the deadline up, Hughie seemed bothered by the sheer scale of the trade rumours. He also lamented, "I read one newspaper story that had twenty-three different names in it."

So what? Surely more than twenty-three names are discussed during the run-up to the trading deadline. Should there be a player-mention cap, modelled after the salary cap? If so, would it increase by a nominal amount each year?

Silly? Sure. But the point is we could have had a good debate like this and it might have been entertaining in its own way. And perhaps, someday, Hughie and I will get together over a couple of beers and have that debate. It seems fairly safe to assume that, from what he tells me about today's NHL, there won't be any players there to interrupt us.

CHAPTER 22

Against the Wall

When the end came for me, it came quickly and unexpectedly. And, in my opinion, unjustly. The season was just getting under way. In fact, it was early October 2009, the Saturday before Canadian Thanksgiving.

Even so, I had already been given my work schedule for the full 2009–10 season. If I remember rightly, I was scheduled to have only three, or possibly four, Saturdays off. During the week, I had been at home in New Brunswick trying to make travel plans for the next three months in order to get flights to Toronto at a reasonable price, either from Saint John or Fredericton. I didn't start to do any work on 2011 flights because I was leaning towards retiring. The commute was getting to be a grind, and the time in Toronto passed slowly, even with the inadvertent entertainment that came along with being a boarder in Christie Blatchford's house.

I had formed a vague plan of doing *Hot Stove* for another month or two and then making up my mind about my future. If I wasn't going to stay, I would leave at the end of December and tell the *Hockey Night* people of my plans around mid-November. It never got that far.

On that pre-Thanksgiving show, which turned out to be my last appearance, we were still discussing Jim Balsillie's plan to purchase the Phoenix Coyotes and relocate the team to Southern Ontario. It wasn't going to work. Balsillie had been far too open about his intentions

201

for Gary Bettman's liking. Worse still, Balsillie had not followed the established procedures required to receive NHL approval for such a move. He had therefore upset Gary Bettman on two fronts, and when you're trying to make headway in the NHL, it's never a good idea to upset Gary Bettman. He will make sure you don't get your way.

When my turn came to chime in on the idea of moving the Coyotes out of Phoenix, I said, "We've seen now it's pretty clear that people in Southern Ontario want another team and would support one, but I can understand that the NHL doesn't want to move one out of there [Arizona].

"The one they may be moving, however—soon, and a lot has been done towards this end—is to move Atlanta to Winnipeg. There is some big money coming out of Toronto that's interested in buying the Thrashers and going through the proper format and going to the governors and applying to move the Atlanta Thrashers there. Now, there is still a lot of work to be done, but there is a lot of work that has been done already."

That was a big story. Up to that point, no one in the media had mentioned the possibility of the Thrashers moving to Winnipeg. The next morning, I was at home fielding phone calls from excited Manitoba news outlets with questions about the report.

But back to Saturday night. After the show finished, I went with Glenn Healy, who had been on the panel that night, over to the Air Canada Centre and ended up having a drink with Jim Hughson and Ron James. I had never met James, who had done some comedy specials on the CBC, but apparently Hughson knew him, and he was good company. We hadn't been there long when Scott Moore, the head of CBC Sports, came over and sat down.

I had taken along a copy of my new book, *Why the Leafs Suck and How They Can Be Fixed*, and it was on the table. Healy picked it up and began reading. The book opens with an account of Toronto Maple Leafs assistant coach Rick Ley trying to teach the team how to set up the trap, the defensive alignment used by many teams at the time. It soon became evident to the players that Ley didn't understand the

concept. Healy laughed and said, "That's exactly right. That's a true story. I was on the ice at the time and we were all laughing about it." Moore picked up the book and looked at its cover. In the lower right was the little CBC pizza that is the corporate logo. "Who said you could use the CBC logo?" asked Moore. I thought he was joking. After all, I figured that anybody who made a living in the media industry would know that the author has nothing to do with the cover design of a book. For that matter, in many cases, the author doesn't even have anything to do with the book's title. In this case, I certainly didn't. I didn't really like the title.

But because I was sure he meant it in a humorous fashion, I responded in kind. "You should be happy about all the free publicity the network will get when the book becomes a bestseller," I said. "You should thank me." Moore did not laugh. Still, he did stay at the table and he wasn't particularly unpleasant—at least no more than is his usual state of being.

On Monday, I was out playing golf when my cell phone rang. It was Sherali Najak. Right away, I knew there was trouble. *Hockey Night in Canada* people don't generally work Mondays. And they definitely don't work Thanksgiving Mondays.

He was calling to tell me that there had been a schedule change and I wouldn't be part of *Hot Stove* on Saturday. He wasn't very specific about the reason. "Something to do with the book," he said. "It was Scott Moore's decision." I said I'd call Moore to see what this was all about. "He's travelling," said Sherali. "I think he's gone to Asia."

The next day, I got a call from the book's publishers, HarperCollins of Canada. The CBC lawyers had called them and expressed unhappiness about the use of the logo. Even though I was not a CBC employee, they were concerned about the implication that anyone who did some contract work at the CBC thought the Leafs sucked.

By Wednesday, the HarperCollins lawyers, who, it seems safe to say, should have been involved in all this long before the cover was sent to print, had now reached an agreement with the CBC. All the books would be recalled from the bookstores; a little white piece of paper would be stuck over the CBC logo; and the books would go back into the stores. So was I now reinstated in the lineup for Saturday's *Hot Stove*? "I have to wait to hear from Scott," said Sherali. "Not this week. Maybe next week."

Saturday came and went. In the middle of the following week, Moore called with the standard going-in-a-different-direction message. I pointed out that firing me for what the publishers put on a book cover was like firing Ron MacLean for a mistake made by the chyron guy. (A chyron is a graphic on the screen, usually at the bottom. I don't know why I used that analogy. I guess it was because I thought that even if Moore didn't know anything about publishing, he might know a little bit about television.)

"It doesn't matter," said Moore. "I'm not having you back."

No one at *Hockey Night*, including Moore, had ever voiced a reasonable complaint about my work on *Hot Stove*. As I mentioned earlier, he had grumbled once about my saying to a newspaper columnist that *Satellite Hot Stove* dealt in gossip, even though the CBC's own website urged viewers to watch it and catch up on "rumors and gossip." But that was behind us and buried.

And in the entire previous season, only one report had proved to be inaccurate. People on shows of that ilk need to be wrong a lot more often than that before a firing is justified. Furthermore, if there had been any doubts about the value of my contributions to the show, surely I would not have been given a schedule requiring me to work almost every Saturday for the next six months. But Moore would give no reason. It was his decision, he said, and it was final.

Not long afterwards, Bill Houston made a reference to it in his "Truth and Rumours" column in the *Globe and Mail*. He wrote that sources confirmed the reason for my leaving *Hot Stove* was tied to my new book, and the CBC logo that appeared on its cover. When that became known, he wrote, "'Scott Moore [the head of CBC Sports and also head of marketing and advertising for the network] went ballistic,' said one insider. Moore's response seems out of character and raises more questions than it answers."

Questions were indeed raised. But answers were not forthcoming. The decision was presumably made because the book upset somebody. But who and why? Could Moore really have been that upset without receiving outside prodding? How was the CBC hurt by having their logo on the book? How was the CBC hurt by the reference to my being from *Hockey Night in Canada*?

Moore was, after all, the head of marketing and advertising for CBC, not for the Toronto Maple Leafs. If a book brings attention to *Hockey Night in Canada*, isn't that good for marketing and advertising?

Could the firing have been an edict from Gary Bettman? Certainly he had the power to get me bounced off *Hockey Night* if he wanted to do so. I asked him about it point-blank. "I didn't get you fired," Bettman said. "If I'd wanted to do that, I would have done it years ago."

I believe Bettman. We are certainly not the closest of friends but we had a degree of respect in our somewhat odd relationship. One year during the Stanley Cup Final, he was in regular attendance and I asked him for his cell phone number. "I'm not going to give you that number," he said. I told him not to be such a pain. "I can get that number if I want it," I said. "I'm just trying to save myself the bother by having you give it to me."

"I don't think you're going to get it anywhere," he replied.

I said, "Look, I'm not going to bother you unduly. Remember when you went off to your cottage for Thanksgiving once and I got that number and called you there because I was onto something important? I never called that number again because I knew if you were there, you were trying to get away."

He was adamant. He wouldn't give me the number. The next day, our paths crossed again. I handed him a slip of paper with his cell number on it.

"I'm not going to call that number because you don't want me to have it," I said. "I'm just letting you know that I'll get your numbers if I want them."

Maybe that was juvenile of me. Then again, maybe it made him respect me a bit more. Who knows? Most probably, he has forgotten all about it. But the point is that as far as I know, he was always straightforward with me.

John Shannon confirmed that Bettman never tried to influence *Hot Stove*. "I never got one call from him or [vice presidents] Steve Solomon or Glenn Adamo about the *Hot Stove*."

After leaving *Hockey Night*, Shannon himself became an NHL vice president, and sometimes mentions were made of the show. Even then, Bettman stayed neutral. "He would just smile about it and say it was entertaining programming," said Shannon.

"We were the gatekeeper of the game in Canada and he had respect for our relationship. He would get mad at Ron every once in a while, but not at us." In simple terms, I don't believe Bettman had anything to do with my firing.

So, I'm guessing the impetus must have come from someone within the Toronto Maple Leafs organization. But really, my book didn't say anything about the Leafs that hadn't already been said. Certainly it recounted their history and made reference to the fact that they hadn't won a Stanley Cup since 1967. It revisited some of their miserable performances over the years, but none of those occurrences had taken place in secret. Their ineptitude was common knowledge. So it seems safe to say that, in the vernacular of the day, the book's title was pretty accurate. They sucked.

Still, that particular reference was only part of the title. It went on to say, "and how they can be fixed." If you read that book and look at the actions the Leafs have followed to make themselves respectable, you'll find they followed my advice. The central theme was that they had to evaluate their situation, determine their assets, and maximize them.

Their biggest asset? Money. They are the richest team in the league, so they should use that advantage, I wrote. That's exactly what they have done. They hired Mike Babcock and gave him $50 million U.S. over eight years, the highest salary of any coach in NHL history. Then, even though they have to pay him the full amount, they fired him after four years when it was determined that he wasn't the man for the job.

They pushed their payroll to the limit mandated under the salary cap—sometimes within a few hundred dollars of the maximum allowed. They made deals with other teams to take on huge contracts belonging to players who were out of hockey, and will never play again, in order to give themselves some more leverage under the convoluted salary cap rules. They boosted their scouting staff. They brought in Brendan Shanahan to act as president and have him under contract until 2025 at a salary believed to be in the $5 million U.S. range. If it isn't the highest in the league, it is very close. So what was so bad about the book?

One thing, certainly, if you're Brian Burke, who was general manager of the Toronto Maple Leafs at the time. It exposed Burke for what he is: a blowhard bully who doesn't come close to living up to the attributes he purports to possess.

The Burke chapter is more than twenty pages long and chronicles his mistakes, blunders, oversights, miscalculations, and outright lies. And it didn't bring any legal action, which, considering Burke's litigious nature, tells you that it is all accurate.

In 2008, Burke showed up in Toronto—after insisting for months that he would not leave his job in Anaheim—and quickly promised that the accepted norm of building a Stanley Cup winner within five years was unacceptable to someone of his talent. He would do it in less. Since he didn't make the playoffs in the four years of his tenure, that promise joined the many over the years that got racked up as nothing more than another burst of Burkean bluster.

But another aspect of Burke's nature is that he tries to get people fired if they disagree with him. He has done it throughout his career with coaches, scouts, and other staffers. He has even done it with media. He got one young man fired from a Vancouver radio job for saying that he found a player's wife attractive.

He tried to get me fired when I said that he was being paid $2 million to be the general manager of the Vancouver Canucks. Joel Darling happened to be in Vancouver that night and Burke stormed up to him and demanded airtime to dispute my claim.

Astonishingly, he got it. "That should never have happened," said John Shannon when we talked about it months later. Burke insisted that the number on the contract designating his pay did not contain a two.

No, but we were talking on Canadian television about a Canadian team. I was talking in Canadian dollars. If the U.S. figure on the contract had been converted to Canadian, it would have hit the $2 million mark.

When Burke was general manager of the Vancouver Canucks, he invited Dennis Skulsky, the publisher of the *Vancouver Province*, to lunch, then launched into an attack on columnist Tony Gallagher and threatened to pull all Canucks advertising from the paper if Gallagher wasn't fired. Skulsky, apparently a man of more resolve than Scott Moore, politely told Burke to mind his own business.

It is worth noting that when all this was going on, Moore regularly socialized with Burke. I was told by a mutual acquaintance that Moore's explanation for my firing was, "I got him on a technicality."

I approached a lawyer after being told of my termination, and he summed it up quickly. He told me that if I were working as an individual, he'd have me back on the show "in a minute." But like most people in similar situations, I had set up a company that hired me, and of which I was the president, which gave me more tax flexibility. It was my company that had the arrangement with the CBC, not me personally, so nothing could be done about it.

These days, Burke, who was given a contract by Moore, is now on Sportsnet, acting as arrogantly as ever. It's a long step down from president of an NHL team to talking head on a sports show. But the move was purely Burke's choice. He himself has told us so.

This much is clear. As the lawyer I consulted pointed out, there were no grounds to fire me and had it not been for the legal technicality—that my company had the contract with CBC and not me—it would have been reversed immediately. I had no history of wrongdoing, something an employer usually requires when releasing an employee. I had no previous consultations with management and I was given no reason for the firing.

Even Scott Moore didn't say I was fired for writing the book. He said he was not bringing me back to *Hot Stove* because the book's publishing company used the CBC logo on the cover, a decision with which I was not involved. And this was a show that was founded on the principle of there being no sacred cows!

CHAPTER 23

Au Revoir

There are lots of love-hate relationships in the world. My relationship with Sherali Najak was love-laugh. I had told him in an email that I was going to call, and the conversation went exactly this way, starting with him foolishly answering a phone that lacks caller ID.

"Hello."

"Here's your big chance to be made famous in a book."

"Wow. You're still alive?"

"Yeah, but judging by the way your show looks these days, I'm not sure you are."

"I suppose I should ask you how you are. [Pause.] Just to pretend that I care."

At this point we were both laughing, so we settled down and got to the matters at hand.

In order for you to understand what follows, I have to give you some insight into Sherali's nature. As you can see, he loves to use insults as a source of humour. And he loves it when people respond in kind. When a lighthearted approach is called for, he's as lighthearted as anyone I've ever met. He can get everyone around him laughing. But when it's time to be serious, he's not only serious, he's insightful, thoughtful, and incisive.

Satellite Hot Stove began as a John Shannon vision. Sherali, who was selected by Shannon to be the show's opening-day director, has

211

always cared deeply about that vision. He shared it wholeheartedly, enriched it, perpetuated it, and finally, with no other options remaining, nursed it into retirement.

For most of my first stretch at *Hot Stove*, Shannon was the executive producer. But when Nancy Lee came in and replaced Shannon with Joel Darling, my days were numbered. In order to fulfill the Shannon vision, the show had to be irreverent, edgy, and even a bit sensational. Inevitably, once those conditions were met, it would stimulate widespread reaction, some of which would be of a critical nature. If that wasn't the case, then the show's initial objective had not been met.

Shannon always had the resolve to face the criticism head-on and stand up to it. So did Najak, who eventually replaced Joel Darling as executive producer and brought me back to the show. But even though Joel's father had once done play-by-play for *Hockey Night in Canada*, he didn't really have any affinity for the show. Like so many others at CBC, he came out of the Ryerson journalism course, and when he was still young, became a highly regarded producer. He was selected to produce the network's CFL games—one of the many CBC sports properties that Nancy Lee lost—and he even worked on the 1988 Olympics.

Over time, Joel evolved into a capable political animal, having learned that at the CBC, it is generally assumed that the less you say, the more you know. His technical expertise as executive producer of *Hockey Night* was not in doubt, but the show, and especially the two contentious intermissions, created its own special kind of off-air problems, which were too much for Joel.

He wanted to keep everyone happy. That was not only impossible, it was an aspect of the job that Joel hated to have to deal with. He never complained about any of my contributions. He just pointed out that he got a lot of letters from people who didn't like my approach. Since I was the one whose actions generated most of the irate phone calls, he reasoned that a great way to ease the negative portion of his workload was to get rid of me. So he did. That was when I left in 2005.

But eventually, even Scott Moore came to the realization that Joel was not the man for the job and moved him out. That was when Sherali came in. Like Joel, Sherali was a CBC veteran, having started at the network long before *Hot Stove* came into being.

"I went to Mohawk College in Hamilton," Sherali said. "I grew up in Hamilton. I was lucky enough that I knew what I wanted to do by the time I was fourteen. My dream was to work for *Hockey Night in Canada* and a big music show. That's what my dream was. Sports and music. I started at the CBC in 1987, but I worked in news and music and entertainment. Then I came to sports in the early nineties.

"There was a big kerfuffle in '94 before the hockey season. There was a big hubbub about this guy coming back to *Hockey Night* and everybody was talking about it. I didn't know John Shannon. He was not a household name for me. I just kept hearing that this guy was coming back to *Hockey Night*. I didn't know about all the past that John went through or about him getting fired for delaying the news, but when he finally came, I saw him in the office one day and I said, 'Hey. I hear you're a big deal.' He thought I was the IT guy. He thought I was there to fix his computer or something. I said, 'Look, I know the building and I've always wanted to work on *Hockey Night*. How can I help you?'

"So the next thing you know, I'm directing the Classics during the '94 lockout. I'm in the control room. Dick Irvin is in there. Don Cherry is in there, and I'm this twenty-something-year-old kid. But I knew what I wanted to be. It was a real good lesson in professionalism and humility and work ethic back in those days. It was really good to go through."

Sherali also worked on the Gretzky Goodwill Tour telecasts, which were used on two Saturday nights during the lockout. Between periods in those games, I was on from Sweden with Ron MacLean. I said to Sherali, "It must have been a real thrill for a kid like you to see me on TV."

"Yeah, it was a real thrill. I thought, 'Wow! This is like Seniors' Corner.'"

"I wasn't *that* old. It was 1995, for Pete's sake."

"True. You just *looked* old."

About a month later, the lockout got settled and *Satellite Hot Stove* made its first appearance on *Hockey Night in Canada*. It was Shannon's baby, and he was producing it, but the director—the guy who determines the cuts from one camera to another—was Sherali. I asked Shannon to put it in layman's terms. "If it were hockey," he said, "the producer is the general manager and the director is the coach." The producer decides which camera feed will go out onto the network, but it is the director who makes sure that the cameras are utilized to give the producer good options.

"I came from the news division at CBC," Najak recalled, "and I thought, 'Oh, I can cut a panel of four guys talking. No problem.' I still remember the first couple of *Hot Stoves* that I was directing. I thought they'd been good, but John was all over me about the way I was cutting it. The thing I started to realize in those early moments was that on *Hot Stove*, we had to deal with a different expectation from the viewers. You needed to show tension. You needed to show body language. It's not like cutting a game, obviously, because that's action, but in terms of the feeling that you were getting from characters on the screen—whether it was JD or you or Eric Duhatschek or Jim Hughson—you could not miss the moments of the eyebrow-raise or the nod. And your eyebrow-raises were one of the highlights of those *Hot Stoves* because it sent a message on the screen to the viewer."

Whether they were the highlight or not is debatable. But they were certainly noticed. Some people called them eye rolls, but there was not much difference between the two. And judging by the people I would meet who would comment on the show, they had evolved into an unintentional trademark.

"There was usually one camera for each person, and then the box to show everybody," Sherali said. "The most important thing to remember was that it wasn't always about what the people were saying. It was also about how the other guys felt when one of the guys was saying what he was saying. You just never wanted to miss any type of feeling that was coming across the screen."

An eye roll—or a raised eyebrow—is an action that doesn't take long to complete. It could easily come and go before a director cut to it. "It's fast," conceded Sherali, "but you have to be dialed in, and you have to rely on your instincts."

"He's absolutely right," said Shannon when we reminisced in 2020. "You have to listen to the content. You have to get a feel for it. When he was directing *Hot Stove*, he had to know that when you said something whacko, JD was going to react, so he had to be ready for that reaction as soon as it occurred."

I would say something whacko? "Yeah, you would," said Shannon. "And it had better be in the book."

"Every single second mattered," Najak said. "That was the thing about *Hockey Night in Canada.* No matter what part of the show you were on, every single second mattered. Nothing was normal. Nothing could ever be regular or normal. Everything had to be special."

Throughout my years on *Hot Stove*, whether it was under Shannon's regime or Najak's, that mind-set was always at the forefront. Before and after the show, there was always fun and camaraderie. When airtime came, focus on the job. Be the best. No excuses.

"I think we were successful most of the time," said Sherali. "I know we always strived. I judged it by how much John yelled at me. If he yelled a lot, then I'd know I wasn't successful."

That was just more Najak humour.

"John's a friend," he said. "He always was. I thought he was a pussy-cat most of the time."

Still, in the early days, Sherali had some uncomfortable moments. He was a young guy working for the master with both of them striving for perfection. But one had the experience; the other didn't.

"There weren't a lot of guys who were directing when John was producing," Sherali said. "I was always the director. Because I was in the office a lot and because I was connected to him a little bit, I gave him the benefit of the doubt because he had a lot of great ideas and I wanted to learn and I knew he cared.

"Also, I grew up in the old CBC news days, working for a lot of different people in the variety division. So I worked for a lot of people who were demanding, but demanding on every level, so I wasn't scared of John the person. I was scared mostly to disappoint. That's where my fear came from: not from John yelling, but from my fear that I had disappointed him."

Still, John was the executive producer and Sherali was invariably being selected as director. John had a long list of candidates, so Sherali must have felt a sense of assurance that he was doing the job properly.

"Yeah, but I was never comfortable," Sherali said. "I never thought about it that way. But in those days, when you're young, you're never thinking about your job, you're thinking about your last show and what you did and how you can do it better. It was always about the product. It was always about the content. Every single conversation was always about what we were doing and why we were doing it. And how we were doing it. And how we were going to do it better."

Most of those conversations were directed towards the intermissions. The number of innovations that can be applied to a game telecast is limited. Not so the intermissions.

"Those were the wallpaper around the game," Sherali said. "The game was so important, but the characters around that stage, that was our brand. That's how we were defined—whether it was the pregame show or the *Coach's Corner* with Don, or the *Hot Stove* with Al and Mike and Ron and all the other characters that we had on. We tried different things in the intermission, too. Those intermission segments had a lot of importance put on them because people listened. People didn't go away for these intermissions. They impacted Canadians sometimes as much as the games did."

Ratings were fairly accurate in those days, and it was clear that the two intermission segments were often outdrawing the games, especially in the regular season.

In an earlier era, when an intermission show consisted of a couple of beer ads used as bookends for a bland interview with a sweaty player, viewers would use the breaks to relieve themselves or get refreshments. Now we had entered a new era. Viewers were sticking around for the intermissions. If the game wasn't exciting, they were liable to go away for extended stretches, but they would make sure that they came back for the intermission show.

It was the golden age of *Satellite Hot Stove*. But when John Shannon left in 2000, it started to slide. Then it slid precipitously during Joel Darling's tenure. It therefore fell to Sherali to try to restore it to its earlier prominence, and for an extended period, *Satellite Hot Stove* struggled to find an identity. There were on-air auditions for personnel, experiments with content, set variations, and many, many format changes.

One of the most obvious alterations was the disappearance of heads in boxes providing views from all over the continent—one of the show's original ideas. *Hot Stove* became a studio show with the panelists sitting side by side or around a table in Toronto.

"There were a few reasons for that," explained Sherali. "I think part of it was the switch to high-definition television. HD affects the audio, so you get a delay if you have someone on location. It's hard to have the kind of conversation we wanted when there's an audio delay, where you can't really jump in. As well, I think part of our decision was we wanted to have more connection between the characters. We moved to studio. That was the biggest reason. In 2008 or so, we moved the entire production into the studio."

Although viewers might not have noticed any difference, the show was no longer prerecorded. Now it was live. Instantaneously live, without the seven-second delay that was imposed on *Coach's Corner* for a while. From our point of view, that was a bit nerve-racking. But to Sherali, who looked at it from a viewpoint of production, it was necessary.

"You remember that we used to record *Coach's Corner* and *Hot Stove* in the afternoons," said Sherali. "That had to evolve. We couldn't go on air with two taped intermissions anymore. Getting it away from the truck [outside the building] because we had multiple games—doing it not from a mobile and doing it from the studio location allowed us to do that.

"The way we had been doing it, both intermissions were basically finished at five o'clock in the afternoon and they were sometimes dated. There was that time, for instance, when there was a twenty-one-player shootout in an afternoon game but both our intermission shows had already been done. We couldn't do anything with it."

Shannon had been gone for years by this point but the foundation that he had created for *Satellite Hot Stove* lived on and was mostly being perpetuated by Sherali, even though the satellite aspect had been left in the dust. There was still the overriding premise that content ruled. Weekday discussions still focused on what was being done and how it could be done better.

"There was a progression that we had to get to," Sherali recalled. "We brought in Brett Hull one time, and I remember it being one of the great moments of the *Hot Stove*. He was with JD in Detroit and he said, 'I'm rich and I'm good looking.' At that time, there were different sets of views that were out there. There were different platforms starting, and we had to figure out, okay, what's the next thing going to be for the viewer? Where are we going? Sometimes, you can't just stay with what you're doing. Sometimes you have to try the new Coke to decide on the old Coke and we did that.

"I remember a lot of pressure coming corporately on the show, and on me as well, to talk less about the business of hockey. I didn't necessarily agree because I think people wanted the scuttlebutt. People wanted that kind of tension. But we had to push ourselves to see what else was out there."

If people didn't want to hear about the business of hockey (a view that was strongly supported by the owners, who didn't want their dubious activities made public), then it would make sense to use some people who had played the game.

"So, we brought in some former players," recalled Sherali. "We talked to different guys."

Most players, once they have left the game, aren't terribly interesting. Furthermore, having been players, they take the approach that what happened in the dressing room should stay in the dressing room. That was the exact opposite of the traditional approach taken by *Hot Stove*. Sherali knew that. He had given it a try in the hope that he might restore the show to prominence, but it simply did not work.

"I remember pulling the plug on it," said Sherali. "I said, 'It's not working. We have to go back.' One of the things I really wanted was Mike Milbury and you. And then I went out and hired Milbury. One of the elements of why I hired Mike was that the success of the first intermission wasn't happening anymore in the second intermission, because we were kind of puttering. The content was out there, but we needed a better way of presenting it, and Mike brought a different opinion to that *Hot Stove* segment. You and he had really good chemistry. He was good and that's when the eyebrow-raise came to the forefront."

Actually, I thought the eyebrow-raise came to the forefront more than a decade earlier, but I didn't want to slow Sherali down at this point. By the time he brought me back to *Hot Stove*, there had been corporate changes. Scott Moore had been named head of CBC Sports. I suggested to Sherali that there must have been a serious difference of opinion when he told Moore of his plan.

"Absolutely," he said. "We had a battle about you coming back, but one of the things that I remember talking to Scott Moore about was this situation. One of the things that I said to him was that the show needed a Strach. It needed somebody that the viewers could yell at, somebody that the viewers would disagree with—or agree with—but we needed that kind of foil."

Here's a good time to remember that television is a numbers game. As long as people are watching, the sponsor doesn't care if they disagree with the person on the screen. It's not a Miss Congeniality contest.

"It's also real life," said Sherali. "When you get a group of sports fans together, do you think they all just look at each other and talk at the right time and are very cordial with each other? No. Somebody is always a smart-ass. And that was you. You were what the show needed at that time and it was the right decision to bring you back—and we had some great moments with you and Mike Milbury. Even when Glenn Healy was there with you. There was some good chemistry and it wasn't always about the information because by then, a lot of the information was out there. It was getting more like it is now. The scoops got fewer and fewer as the platform changed, so we had to evolve. We couldn't rely on just the main platform. We had to be leaning on that, but what we had to evolve to was presenting different opinions as opposed to just information."

Milbury and I had our disagreements on the air. We had them off the air, too, for that matter. Our personalities are such that we remained friends, but people loved the on-air battles.

"The reason people accepted it is because there was still some authenticity to it," said Sherali. "If you just yelled at each other, it wouldn't have worked. And that was something that was really important to me. We didn't want it to be fully about you yelling at each other because that wasn't *Hockey Night*. It had to be under the umbrella of the brand, which was authenticity and having an opinion, and being hard, and your convictions about it. I chalked it up to needing the eyebrow-raise. The viewer just wants to feel something. Just make them feel something by not being phony about it. That's the fine line that we had to make sure we never crossed—by trying to manufacture stuff.

"You had to have the right characters in place, then you didn't have to manufacture things. There was a level of respect, but not everybody had to agree with each other. We had a lot of pressure on those intermissions. Those intermissions had to deliver, on a big scale."

So for a while, circa 2008, ratings were jumping and people were talking about the show again. To the viewing audience, at least, *Hot Stove* was back to being what Shannon called the original version: "appointment television." It had also moved on from being disappointment television.

It might better have been called duck television: progressing smoothly on the surface but paddling like hell underneath.

"I got complaint phone calls all the time," Sherali said.

I suggested that the most active caller in that regard was probably Brian Burke.

"Brian was definitely one of them," conceded Sherali, "but it was across the league, from owners to GMs—and I'm sure John Shannon got them, too, before me. Everybody bitched about something that was said.

"I remember going out and sitting down with two of the governors of Canadian teams out west," recalled Sherali. "Twice I went out and sat down for the afternoon and we talked about what was said and what their complaints were. I ended up basically defending what we were doing and stressing that we could not relinquish our editorial control. We just couldn't do it. Our autonomy could not be sold.

"You'd fly out for the day, and I didn't mind having these face-to-face meetings. They're allowed to say what they want. That's part of the relationship. But we had to do what we felt was right for the show and that meant doing it with respect—everything with respect.

"*Hockey Night in Canada* was always separate from the league. We had autonomy. We were able to have our own opinions and we weren't really manipulated or controlled by anybody. Back in the day, we were very different."

But it didn't stop NHL people at the team management level complaining and trying to influence the show. In fact, that different status that *Hockey Night* enjoyed probably encouraged the complainers.

"I think the owners and GMs complained when they were being talked about," said Sherali. "And when they weren't being talked about. That's what I think. It was a big deal to make it onto *Hot Stove* in those days."

It seems certain that if team presidents were complaining to Sherali Najak, they were also complaining to Gary Bettman. There's no doubt that Bettman could have cracked down on that show in a minute. He never interfered.

"Nobody interfered, and it was respectful on both sides," Sherali said. "We were very respectful of the league, but we had a voice and I think the viewers appreciated that because it was like reading a column in the newspaper. It was all the special columnists that you read all the time in the paper. Now they were on the screen in front of you."

But suddenly, without any previous suggestion that my work was unacceptable, I was "suspended." Indefinitely. This was a touchy subject. Moore hadn't seen fit to call me himself. He had given Sherali the job of passing the news to me.

"Scott is a friend so I want to leave it there," he said. "And I see your eyebrow raising right now."

"So you want me to say you refused to comment?"

Sherali did not. He is, after all, in the news-dissemination business, where everyone else is expected to comment.

So I persevered. "So why did I get fired?"

"I don't believe he was happy with some of the stuff that you said, so that stirred the pot a little bit. It helps when you don't stir the pot."

I said, "But that's what you hired me to do."

"I know."

I pushed the matter a little further. "Did you try to get Moore's decision overturned?"

"God, are you kidding? I was happy you were gone."

We were both laughing. Sherali said, "You know what I like about our relationship, Strach? It's that we're different people, different backgrounds, and we can say anything to each other and I appreciate that.

"The answer is that he knew where I stood on it, obviously, because I had hired you back. But my bullets had all been used. He knew that I wanted you back not only for our relationship, but also for the show. It was the best thing for the show to have different types of characters. You can't have the same people on all the time. It was the start of a different show," said Sherali. "It was probably the start of the end."

Conclusion

We're now at the point where I'm supposed to sum it all up. It's time to give you all the highlights and lowlights. But really, the only lowlight was when I got fired for the second and final time.

I doubt that I would have stayed on after that season, but I would have preferred to have left on my terms—or at least for having done something so outrageous that there was no choice in the matter, or something memorable like the Dave Hodge pen flip.

Other than that, *Hot Stove* was a wonderful experience. Obviously, the segment had its detractors. What doesn't? But it had a hell of a lot more supporters. That's why people who know the publishing industry feel there's a market for this book even though the show is long gone.

John Davidson hit the nail on the head with his capsule comment about his involvement with the show. I hope it was sufficiently clear that he spoke identical sentences with a different inflection.

"It was *Hockey Night in Canada*," he said, using a tone that implied admiration for the show. "And it was hockey night in Canada," meaning it was Saturday night and for decades, from coast to coast in Canada, this show had been an integral part of the social fabric.

Its coverage of the National Hockey League started the same year that Maple Leaf Gardens opened. It had outlasted the Montreal Maroons, the Brooklyn Americans, the Kansas City Scouts, the Colorado Rockies, and the Cleveland Barons. (I could go on for a while, but I think you've got the picture.)

For about fifteen years, *Hot Stove* was one of *Hockey Night in Canada*'s main attractions. It had its controversial moments, but it always dealt with both sides of the story. Whether it was a rule proposal, a new league policy, an officiating decision, or an issue pitting players against management, whatever was hot that week was debated on *Hot Stove*, with both sides getting their due. And in many cases, the issue in the spotlight was one that the public didn't know about until someone on the *Hot Stove* panel exposed it.

One Saturday evening during the playoffs, I was in Edmonton. The Oilers weren't playing that night and I was staying across the street from the Northlands Coliseum. There was an Aerosmith concert going on, so I went over to watch some of it (from the penalty box as I explained earlier). To me, Aerosmith is one of those groups that had some great songs, but you don't want to listen to them all night. After I heard "Dream On," I decided to leave. As I was walking along the empty concourse under the stands towards the arena exit, Aerosmith lead singer Steven Tyler suddenly emerged from one of the passages, coming towards me, trailing his robes and scarves behind him. Perhaps the inevitable drum solo had begun. Tyler was literally bouncing and as we passed, he gave a fist pump and shouted to me, "That was great, wasn't it?" I agreed that it was.

I knew how he felt. I think that with very few exceptions, we all felt that way every time Ron wrapped up *Hot Stove*. We were exhilarated. We felt good about what we had done. We believed that we had told viewers something they had not previously known and we were convinced that they had enjoyed what they had seen. Sure, we were sometimes a bit miffed after the show that Ron hadn't got to one of the points we wanted to raise, but we invariably felt that despite that, we had provided good television.

Once in a long while, we weren't quite as euphoric, but those occasions were rare. I remember saying once, "Well, it's an inescapable fact that no matter how good the shows are, one of them has to be the worst of the season. I think that one was it." I don't remember the particulars, but it was probably a show involving Rick Westhead.

And the enthusiasm was definitely tempered the night that we had learned that Scott Morrison's wife, Kathy, was suffering from terminal brain cancer. On that occasion, we had taken the elevator up to the studio from Sherali Najak's office and on the way, said something to each other about living up to our responsibilities. No one watching that show would have known from our actions that a little while before it started, we had been in tears.

Perhaps some of the post-show euphoria was an emotional release. We were always a little tense before the show, especially if it was live. You try not to think that more than a million people are watching, and that if you make a stupid mistake you're stuck with it. You don't get a do-over.

There were never any scripts on that show. There was an outline listing potential topics, but as has been frequently mentioned, it existed in a purely advisory capacity. You're on live television, trying to craft your words so that your point is made succinctly and accurately. As you're saying one sentence, you're already formulating another, and if you start a sentence incorrectly, you have to quickly make a mental deletion of what you were going to say and find a new set of words to complete the sentence. It's a linguistic mental gymnastics, and if you do it right, the sentences should flow.

To my mind, if you are listening to a sports reporter being interviewed on the radio and he peppers his comments with "you know," or "er," or "like"—or all of them—you have every right to be annoyed, as well as skeptical. Language is the primary tool of his craft. If he can't wield it more skillfully than that, you have to wonder about the manner in which he does the rest of his job.

I think it's safe to say that on *Hot Stove*, all the regulars made points well. But it's not as easy as it seems. When the shows ended, there was that release that comes with having cleared another hurdle—the feeling of "Hey! We did it again!"

Or, as John Shannon once put it, "There's no better feeling than creating great TV."

Acknowledgments

When Simon & Schuster asked me to write this book, I responded with a conditional agreement. "I'll do it if John Shannon will cooperate," I said.

I knew that if there were no outside factors in play—such as John doing a book of his own—I'd be able to count on his help. As it turned out, he is doing a book of his own. But that didn't stop him being a tremendous help to me. He was not only the creator of *Hot Stove* as we know it, he was its driving force, so without him my book would be a shadow of what it turned out to be. But he answered every question, filled in every blank, and, more than once, even corrected what I had got wrong.

As might be expected, the two women in my life also helped me put it all together. Marian Strachan lives in Lancashire, and when not combatting the effects of gales coming in off the Irish Sea, did her usual superb job of editing my copy before it went to the publisher. Lucie Leduc lives with me and put up with my usual bouts of intransigence, lethargy, and stubbornness to keep me returning to the computer.

There are countless others whose efforts I appreciate—so many that the list is too long to fit into the allotted space. But if you're quoted in the book, then you helped, and for that, I thank you.

I must also mention that it was a delight to work with Justin Stoller, the editor who apparently drew the short straw at Simon & Schuster and got assigned to work on the book. My good friend Christie Blatchford, who died while the book was in its formative stages, liked to say that "editors are the kind of people who watch the battle from the hills, then come down and rob the bodies." Justin, I'm delighted to say, was not even close to being that kind of editor.

And although literary agents might be expected to have a firm grasp of the English language, Brian Wood seems unable to comprehend such simple statements as "No" and "I am retired." Nevertheless, he's a fine agent and I'm glad to have him on my side.

There probably will be mistakes. In one of my earlier books, I managed to get my son Andrew's birth date wrong and Marian, his mother, didn't catch it. But the mistake was mine and any that pop up in this book will also be mine. I accept full responsibility.